WELCOME TO RUNEQUEST

THIS QUICKSTART ADVENTURE INTRODUCES THE RUNEQUEST system and the world of Glorantha. It is intended to be played with a group of 3–6 players and one gamemaster. To play this adventure, you, the gamemaster, should hand out the pregenerated adventurers (pages 42–47), assigning them as desired. Familiarize yourself with the rules until you're comfortable with them. You should have at least one set of dice as described under the *Materials* section nearby, and something to write with. The map on page 27 is also useful as a handout, but not essential.

INTRODUCING GLORANTHA

If the players are unfamiliar with Glorantha, you should read or paraphrase the following to them, providing a brief overview of Glorantha and this particular part of the world.

Welcome to Glorantha, a heroic, mythic place of heroes and gods, where people hold allegiance to tribe, city, and cult, not to abstract alignments or ideologies. Although humanity is the dominant species, their dominance is due only to the quarrelling of the Elder Races, who still rule large parts of the world.

In Glorantha, the gods and goddesses are real, and through their cults they play an important role in most major events. Would-be heroes of the age are known as adventurers, and each is tied to several of the Runes, cosmic powers that define Glorantha and are likewise manifested by the gods. Powerful deities are associated with the Sun, Earth, Air, Water, Darkness, and the Moon, as well as with Death, Life, Change, Stasis, Illusion, Truth, Disorder, and Harmony, and each has its Rune. Adventurers join the cults of their gods, from which they get magic and aid.

Adventurers are participating and active members of society, whether clan, tribe, city, or other community. They have duties, loyalties, and conflicts beyond being mere freebooters, with ties to the world of Glorantha and the Runes as deep as they are profound. As adventurers advance within their cults, they strengthen their connection to the Runes, gaining power and questing towards becoming true Heroes.

One of the most important places in all of Glorantha is Dragon Pass, located in the heart of the great continent of Genertela. It is a land beset by conflict and blessed with opportunity, an extremely magical place, center of many of the world's great myths, and Dragon Pass is prophesied to be the site of the great, apocalyptic series of events called the Hero Wars. A recent revolution against the occupying Lunar Empire has left many of the cities of Dragon Pass in ruins. Nobles, cults, and clans vie for power and authority in their wake, and its liberators struggle to rebuild and reclaim that which was lost.

MATERIALS

To play this adventure you will need an assortment of dice, particularly the 10 (D10) or 20-sided dice (D20), the 8-sided dice (D8), the 6-sided dice (D6), and the 4-sided dice (D4). Dice designations may be preceded by a number. For instance, 2D6 requires that two 6-sided dice be rolled.

Whenever a result of more than one die is called for, add the results together to form a single total.

Sometimes additions are made to specified die rolls. Add the number following the plus sign to the result of the roll, so that 1D6+1 means rolling a D6 and adding 1, and for 1D4–2 you roll the D4 and subtract 2 from the total. Occasionally specified die rolls require that different dice be rolled at one time. If a weapon does 1D6+2D4 damage, for instance, the actual damage is found by rolling the three requested dice and adding their results. Always round up when it benefits the players, and round down when it is detrimental to them. If the result is less than 0, consider the final result as 0.

The most important dice for RUNEQUEST is the D100, or percentile dice. To generate a D100 result, roll a D10 twice. The first roll is the "tens" roll, and the second is the "ones." Thus if you roll a 5 the first time, and an 8 the second time, you've rolled 58. A dice roll of "00" equals 100. Some D10 dice are numbered as tens (10, 20, 30, etc.). Such dice should be used as the "tens" roll, and a normal D10 then can be used for the "ones." In such cases, a roll of "00" (tens) and "0" (ones) means a result of 100.

Less common are the D3 or D2, created by rolling a D6 and dividing by two (for D3) or by three (for a D2).

Yanioth, Vareena's Daughter

THE GAME SYSTEM

CHARACTERISTICS

At the heart of RuneQuest are characters, either adventurers (those controlled by players) or non-player characters (other humans and creatures controlled by the gamemaster). All characters—whether adventurers, non-player characters, monsters, spirits, or anything else—are defined by some or all of the same seven characteristics. The higher the characteristic, the better.

- **Strength (STR):** Raw strength, determining damage bonus, how much can be carried, what weapons can be wielded, etc.
- **Constitution (CON):** Health and stamina, determining hit points and healing rate (see page 18), ability to stay conscious when badly wounded, and to resist disease and poison.
- **Size (SIZ):** Physical mass (height and/or weight), determining hit points, damage bonus, and strike rank in combat.
- **Dexterity (DEX):** Speed and physical reflexes, influencing physical activities such as fighting, dodging, and strike rank in combat.
- **Intelligence (INT):** Reasoning, memory, problem-solving, inspiration, knowledge, also useful for some kinds of magic.
- **Power (POW):** Spiritual presence, willpower, and luck, indicating favor from the universe and the gods. Determines magic points, used when casting spells.
- **Charisma (CHA):** Leadership and force of personality, determining how willing others are to be influenced, whether through charm or menace. Influences the amount of Rune magic available and how many spirit magic spells can be possessed.

ABILITY USE

Most important actions require the use of a particular ability, defined as a **skill**, **Rune**, or **passion**. Abilities are functions that anyone can perform. For actions anyone can accomplish without difficulty (getting up, getting dressed, eating, etc.), an adventurer is assumed to automatically succeed, meaning no ability roll is required.

In most cases, determining the chance of success for any given action is very easy in RuneQuest. Most adventurer abilities, including skills, are expressed as a percentile chance of success on a D100 (abilities with a rating of "00" have zero **chance of success**). The adventurer sheet shows the chances of success for most actions.

For any ability performed in a dramatic circumstance, an ability roll is required. It is usually obvious when an **ability roll** should be made, but if in doubt, the gamemaster should consider the consequences of failure. If the chance of failure heightens tension, makes things exciting, and if failure will add fun to the game, the gamemaster should have the player make an ability roll.

AUGMENTING ABILITIES

Where appropriate, abilities—whether Runes, skills, or passions—may be combined to **augment** one another, using one ability in support of another. The abilities to be combined must be clearly relevant to the task at hand, and are subject to the gamemaster's approval. *For example, a Love (Family) passion might augment a Search roll when looking for a clue to the whereabouts of a missing brother.* Only one ability can augment another for any given roll.

To augment one ability with another, first roll for the ability being used in support of the other.

- **Critical Success:** Add +50% to the desired ability.
- **Special Success:** Add +30% to the desired ability.
- **Success:** Add +20% to the desired ability.
- **Failure:** Subtract –20% from the desired ability.
- **Fumble:** Subtract –50% from the desired ability.

This modifier is applied to the chance of success for the primary roll, before the primary roll is attempted. An adventurer can even augment the casting chance of a spell through ritual practices or abilities such as Dance, Sing, Meditation, etc.

Abilities may also be used to augment rolls on the resistance table (see page 6), again at the gamemaster's discretion. Adventurers can help each other in the same fashion, using skills in support of other adventurer's skill roll, with the gamemaster's approval.

ABILITIES ABOVE 100%

In some instances, such as when augmenting, an ability might increase beyond 100%, though the adventurer still has no better than a 95% of succeeding.

- If the opponent is trying to parry, block, dodge, or otherwise oppose the character's use of the ability, then 100%+ ability gives a greater chance of overcoming the opposition. If the highest rated participant in an opposed resolution has an ability rating in excess of 100%, the difference between 100 and their ability rating is subtracted from the ability of everyone in the contest (including themselves).
- While actual chance of success remains no better than 95%, the chance of a special or critical success continues to increase.

REATTEMPTING ABILITY ROLLS

An adventurer failing an ability roll may still be in a situation where they could potentially try again or where there has been some significant change in circumstances. The gamemaster may permit a follow-up attempt, but at a –25% penalty. If this second attempt fails, the adventurer cannot make any further reattempts without the passage of time or change in circumstances. This does not apply to combat rolls.

CHARACTERISTIC ROLLS

When an action attempted is not an ability, the gamemaster can use a characteristic roll. Usually these equal the value of the characteristic ×5. This can be increased or decreased for different circumstances, from simple (×10) to almost impossible (×1). Following are some examples:

- **Strength Check (STR×5):** Intense muscular efforts like bashing a door open, carrying someone, etc.
- **Constitution Check (CON×5):** Resisting illnesses, poisons, etc., or during intense or prolonged effort (long run, etc.).
- **Intelligence Check (INT×5):** Testing memory or logic, deduction, recalling somebody's face or name, etc.
- **Dexterity Check (DEX×5):** Resolving actions requiring good coordination, physical or manual skill, speed or balance (catching a thrown object, walking on a roof, etc.).
- **Luck Check (POW×5):** Determining if the adventurer catches a lucky break, or has a stroke of good fortune when the odds could go either way.
- **Charisma Check (CHA×5):** Resolving verbal or non-verbal social contests where skills (such as Bargain, Charm, Fast Talk, Intimidate, Intrigue, or Orate) do not apply.

RESULTS

Whenever resolving some form of contest using an ability, try to roll equal to or under the ability's rating (the chance of success) with a D100, consulting the **Ability Results** table (nearby) for the exact result. Always use the best result indicated by the dice roll. Possible results are as follows, ranging from best to worst:

- **Critical Success:** A task performed exceptionally well gains extra benefits. A critical success is an ability roll of 5% (1/20) or less of the modified chance of success. A roll of 01 is always a critical success. The benefit of any critical success depends on the ability being used: weapons ignore armor, climbers gain extra distance, crafters make extra valuable goods, etc. In an opposed resolution, a critical success is always better than a normal or special success.
- **Special Success:** In some cases, an ability roll result that is better than usual, but not a critical success, can have additional benefits. A special success is an ability roll of 20% (1/5) or less of the modified chance of success. As with the critical success, the special success is based on the modified chance of success, not on the user's raw ability rating. In an opposed resolution, a special success is always better than a normal success.

ABILITY RESULTS

Ability	Critical	Special	Success	Fail	Fumble
01–05	01	01	01–05	06–00	96–00
06–07	01	01	Per ability	Per ability	96–00
08–10	01	01–02	Per ability	Per ability	96–00
11–12	01	01–02	Per ability	Per ability	97–00
13–17	01	01–03	Per ability	Per ability	97–00
18–22	01	01–04	Per ability	Per ability	97–00
23–27	01	01–05	Per ability	Per ability	97–00
28–29	01	01–06	Per ability	Per ability	97–00
30	01–02	01–06	Per ability	Per ability	97–00
31–32	01–02	01–06	Per ability	Per ability	98–00
33–37	01–02	01–07	Per ability	Per ability	98–00
38–42	01–02	01–08	Per ability	Per ability	98–00
43–47	01–02	01–09	Per ability	Per ability	98–00
48–49	01–02	01–10	Per ability	Per ability	98–00
50	01–03	01–10	Per ability	Per ability	98–00
51–52	01–03	01–10	Per ability	Per ability	99–00
53–57	01–03	01–11	Per ability	Per ability	99–00
58–62	01–03	01–12	Per ability	Per ability	99–00
63–67	01–03	01–13	Per ability	Per ability	99–00
68–69	01–03	01–14	Per ability	Per ability	99–00
70	01–04	01–14	Per ability	Per ability	99–00
71–72	01–04	01–14	Per ability	Per ability	00
73–77	01–04	01–15	Per ability	Per ability	00
78–82	01–04	01–16	Per ability	Per ability	00
83–87	01–04	01–17	Per ability	Per ability	00
88–89	01–04	01–18	Per ability	Per ability	00
90–92	01–05	01–18	Per ability	Per ability	00
93–95	01–05	01–19	Per ability	Per ability	00
96–97	01–05	01–19	01–95	96–00	00
98–100	01–05	01–20	01–95	96–00	00
(higher)	5% ability	20% ability	01–95	96–00	00

- **Success:** A result of equal to or less than the ability's rating indicates that the task succeeded. A roll of 01–05 on D100 is always a success, even if the ability rating is lower.
- **Failure:** A result of greater than the ability's rating (with any modifiers factored in) indicates failure. A roll of 96–00 is always a failure, even if the ability rating is higher.
- **Fumble:** A spectacularly bad attempt is a fumble, equal to 5% of the chance of failure. The chance for a fumble depends on the modified percentage roll for the situation,

ADVENTURER OVERVIEW

Take a look at the pregenerated character sheets at the back of this quickstart, you will see that they are made up of many different parts.

1. BACKGROUND

The adventurer's background and personal history.

2. CHARACTERISTICS

Adventurers are defined by seven characteristics, described on pages 2-3.

3. MAGIC POINTS AND SPIRIT MAGIC

How many magic points the adventurer can use to cast spirit magic with, and (in the second column) what spells they can cast. Spirit Magic is described on pages 18.

4. HIT LOCATIONS

The adventurer's hit locations. When the adventurer is struck successfully by an attack, roll a D20 to determine where it hits. Each hit location's armor and hit points are presented like so: (Armor)/(Hit Points). See page 17 for more information on hit points and damage.

5. WEAPONS

The weapons or shield carried by the adventurer, described by name, skill percentage, damage dice, strike rank, and the weapon's hit points. Ranged weapons have Range presented also. See page 13 for more information about weapons and page 7 for a description of how strike ranks work.

6. RUNES

The Runes the adventurer is most aligned with. Runes are described on page 8.

7. PASSIONS

Things the adventurer feels strongly about, such as loyalties, family, kin, honor, etc. Passions are described on page 10.

8. MOVE

Most humans move at the same rate, defined as MOV units. Movement is described on page 8.

9. DAMAGE BONUS

Add this bonus to all hand-to-hand attacks, and add half this bonus (roll and divide) into thrown weapons. It has already been added into the adventurer weapon descriptions.

10. SPIRIT COMBAT DAMAGE

This determines how much damage your adventurer can do when in combat with spirits. See page 19 for more information on spirit combat.

11. STRIKE RANKS

Attack speeds are ordered by Strike Ranks, based on Dexterity (DEX) and SIZ (SIZ). Strike Ranks are described on page 7.

12. HIT POINTS

How many hit points the adventurer has, in total. Mark these off when the adventurer takes damage. See page 17 for more information on hit points and damage.

13. ARMOR

The armor protecting the adventurer, per location. Armor is subtracted from damage done to that hit location. See page 17 for more information on armor.

14. SKILLS AND LANGUAGES

The adventurer's skills and their ratings. The bonuses to these are skill category modifiers, and are already calculated into the skill totals. Skills are described on pages 11.

15. RUNE POINTS AND RUNE SPELLS

How many Rune Points the adventurer has in their cult, and the Rune spells the adventurer can cast with those points. Rune Points and Rune spells are described on pages 20-24.

16. TREASURES AND MAGIC ITEMS

Any small items of worth the adventurer has, along with their values in Lunars (L). and any magic items and their properties, if any. The primary unit of money is the Lunar (L) a silver coin. A free family can live for a year on 60 L or so.

REPUTATION AND RANSOM

These two values play an important part in many RuneQuest campaigns, but are not hugely relevant to *The Broken Tower*. **Reputation** measures how well-known the adventurer is, rated as the chance someone will have heard of them. The higher, the more famous. **Ransom** is the amount in Lunars (L) that the adventurer's family and clan will pay if the adventurer is captured.

MOUNT/ALLY/CREATURE

Some adventurers have mounts, allies, or creatures they can summon. These are controlled by the adventurers, though successful skill rolls (Ride, etc.) may be required to control them in combat or other stressful situations. See separate write-ups on pages 47-48 for more information on each adventurer's mount or elemental.

VASANA, DAUGHTER OF FARNAN

Veteran heavy cavalrywoman of the Ernaldori clan of the Colymar Tribe.
Female, age 21. Initiate of Orlanth Adventurous.

Introduction: *I am Vasana, the daughter of Farnan, a hero of Starbrow's Rebellion, slain and devoured by the Crimson Bat. In my war of revenge against the Lunar Empire, I gained the attention of Argrath at the Battle of Pennel Ford. I was sorely wounded at the Second Battle of Moonbroth, granting me this terrible scar across on the left half of my face. I returned to my mother's farm to recover, and now I am ready for adventure. My friends know me for a fearsome bison rider, a skilled hand with a sword, and a devout worshipper of Orlanth Adventurous. My honor is my greatest strength.*

Vasana is a small but athletic woman with red-hair and a vicious scar across her left face. Despite her small size, she rides a bison and is more than capable of commanding warriors and priests more senior than herself.

Vasana's grandmother was a scribe in the service of the Princes of Sartar, and died with great glory in the Battle of Boldhome. Vasana's father was Farnan, a temple orphan who married Vareena, a priestess of Ernalda from the Ernaldori clan. Farnan joined Starbrow's Rebellion and later personally aided Kallyr Starbrow in her escape from Sartar. He died defending Whitewall in 1620, devoured by the Crimson Bat. Farnan's soul was annihilated and Vasana, then a teenager, swore revenge.

As soon as she was initiated as an adult, Vasana left her mother's farm to avenge her father against the Lunar Empire. In 1623, she followed King Broyan to the metropolis of Nochet, accompanied by her half-sister Yanioth. At the Battle of Pennel Ford, she fought with great glory, and gained the attention of Argrath. Vasana followed Argrath into Prax and joined the army of the White Bull in the liberation of Pavis. Pursuing honor again, she fought with great glory at the Second Battle of Moonbroth, and was nearly killed (receiving a nasty scar across her left eye) in the process of killing a Lunar priestess. After the Dragonrise, she returned to her mother's farm to recover.

STR 16	CON 12	SIZ 10
INT 15	DEX 11	CHA 19
POW 14	Magic Points: 14	

Location	D20	Armor/HP
Right Leg	01–04	5/4
Left Leg	05–09	5/4
Abdomen	09–11	3/4
Chest	12	5/5
Right Arm	13–15	5/3
Left Arm	16–18	5/3
Head	19-20	5/4

Weapon	%	Damage	SR	Pts
Broadsword	90	1D8+1+1D4	7	12
Lance	70	1D10+1+3D6	6	10
Battle Axe	55	1D8+2+1D4	7	10
Medium Shield	65	1D6+1D4	7	12
Composite Bow	45	1D8+1	3	7

Runes: Air 90% (Ⓖ), Moon 90% (Φ), Earth 20% (□), Death 75% (†), Truth 70% (Ⅱ), Movement 75% (ʒ).

Passions: Hate (Lunar Empire) 90%, Honor 90%, Devotion (Orlanth) 80%, Loyalty (Sartar) 80%, Loyalty (Argrath) 70%, Loyalty (Colymar Tribe) 70%.

Reputation: 20%
Ransom: 500 L.

Move: 8
Damage Bonus: +1D4
Spirit Combat Damage: 1D6+3
Strike Ranks: DEX 3, SIZ 2
Hit Points: 12
Armor: Bronze disk plate cuirass (5 pts.), bronze greaves and vambraces (5 pts.), studded leather skirt (3 pts.), closed helm (5 pts.).
Skills: *Agility:* Dodge 22%, Ride (Bison) 70%. *Communication:* Dance 25%, Orate 45%, Sing 50%. *Knowledge:* Battle 65%, Cult Lore (Orlanth) 25%, Customs (Heortling) 35%, Farm 30%, First Aid 25%, Herd 20%. Manipulation +5% (includes all weapon skills). *Magic:* Meditate 25%, Spirit Combat 55%, Worship (Orlanth) 35%. *Perception:* Listen 40%, Scan 50%, Search 30%, Track 10%. *Stealth +5%:* Hide 15%, Move Quietly 15%.
Languages: Speak Heortling 60%, Speak Stormspeech 34%, Speak Tradetalk 20%, Read/Write Theyalan 30%, Read/Write New Pelorian 15%.
Rune Points: 3 (Orlanth Adventurous)
Rune Spells: Command Cult Spirit (2), Dark Walk (1), Dismiss Magic (Var.), Dismiss Air Elemental (as per elemental size), Divination (1), Earth Shield (3), Extension 1, Find Enemy 1, Flight (var.), Heal Wound (1), Leap (1), Lightning (var.), Mist Cloud (1), Multispell (1), Shield (var.), Spirit Block (var.), Summon Air Elemental (as per elemental size, see separate write-up), Teleportation (3), Wind Words (1).
Spirit Magic: Mobility (1 pt.), Demoralize (2 pts.), Healing 2.
Magic Items: 10-point magic point storage crystal, piece of raw Truestone.
Treasures: Carries 20 L in coin, armor and helmet, medium shield, broadsword, lance, battle axe, composite bow with 20 arrows, riding bison (see separate write-up).

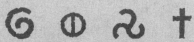

not on the normal chance with the ability. A fumble is the worst possible failure and usually has disastrous consequences. In an opposed resolution, a fumble is always worse than a failure.

OPPOSED RESOLUTION

Opposed rolls are made when one character's ability is pitched against an opponent's ability. A simple success may not be enough to overcome the opponent. Opposed rolls are not used to resolve melee combat.

To make an opposed roll, both participants roll their respective abilities. If both participants succeed, the winner is whoever rolled higher. If one participant got a special success and the other a normal success, the special success is the winner. If one participant got a critical success and the other a normal or special success, the critical success is the winner.

An opposed resolution may thus result in a winner and a loser, a tie, or two losers.

- **Winner and a Loser:** The winner succeeds and the loser fails.
- **Tie:** A tie (where both participants succeed but roll the same number) means the situation is temporarily unresolved. If both participants rolled a critical success, the result is a tie.
- **Two Losers:** Both participants fail their rolls. Stalemate, no success.

THE RESISTANCE TABLE

Sometimes an action depends on one raw characteristic overcoming an obstacle. Use a **resistance roll** to resolve these situations. Resistance rolls are not used for skill, Rune, or passion rolls. They are used when pitting one characteristic against another, such as STR against the SIZ of an object to be lifted or the magic points of a spellcaster against the magic points of their target to see if the spell overcame the target's resistance.

When using a resistance roll one characteristic is defined as active and the other passive. The active exerts influence on the passive. The formula for overcoming resistance is: **% of success = 50% plus (active ×5%) minus (passive ×5%).** If equal, there is a 50% chance of success. As usual, a roll of 01–05 always succeeds, and a roll of 96–00 always fails. As with other rolls, resistance rolls may result in critical successes, special successes, and fumbles.

The **Resistance Table** (below) puts the resistance roll formula into an easy-to-use reference. The number indicated is the percentage needed for success. A line indicates there is no chance of success other than on a roll of 01–05.

RESISTANCE TABLE

POW of Attacking Force

POW of Defending Force	01	02	03	04	05	06	07	08	09	10	11	12	13	14	15	16	17	18	19	20	21
01	50	55	60	65	70	75	80	85	90	95	—	—	—	—	—	—	—	—	—	—	—
02	45	50	55	60	65	70	75	80	85	90	95	—	—	—	—	—	—	—	—	—	—
03	40	45	50	55	60	65	70	75	80	85	90	95	—	—	—	—	—	—	—	—	—
04	35	40	45	50	55	60	65	70	75	80	85	90	95	—	—	—	—	—	—	—	—
05	30	35	40	45	50	55	60	65	70	75	80	85	90	95	—	—	—	—	—	—	—
06	25	30	35	40	45	50	55	60	65	70	75	80	85	90	95	—	—	—	—	—	—
07	20	25	30	35	40	45	50	55	60	65	70	75	80	85	90	95	—	—	—	—	—
08	15	20	25	30	35	40	45	50	55	60	65	70	75	80	85	90	95	—	—	—	—
09	10	15	20	25	30	35	40	45	50	55	60	65	70	75	80	85	90	95	—	—	—
10	05	10	15	20	25	30	35	40	45	50	55	60	65	70	75	80	85	90	95	—	—
11	—	05	10	15	20	25	30	35	40	45	50	55	60	65	70	75	80	85	90	95	—
12	—	—	05	10	15	20	25	30	35	40	45	50	55	60	65	70	75	80	85	90	95
13	—	—	—	05	10	15	20	25	30	35	40	45	50	55	60	65	70	75	80	85	90
14	—	—	—	—	05	10	15	20	25	30	35	40	45	50	55	60	65	70	75	80	85
15	—	—	—	—	—	05	10	15	20	25	30	35	40	45	50	55	60	65	70	75	80
16	—	—	—	—	—	—	05	10	15	20	25	30	35	40	45	50	55	60	65	70	75
17	—	—	—	—	—	—	—	05	10	15	20	25	30	35	40	45	50	55	60	65	70
18	—	—	—	—	—	—	—	—	05	10	15	20	25	30	35	40	45	50	55	60	65
19	—	—	—	—	—	—	—	—	—	05	10	15	20	25	30	35	40	45	50	55	60
20	—	—	—	—	—	—	—	—	—	—	05	10	15	20	25	30	35	40	45	50	55
21	—	—	—	—	—	—	—	—	—	—	—	05	10	15	20	25	30	35	40	45	50

The number indicated is the percentage needed for success.

TIME & MOVEMENT

Game time is fictitious and has little to do with passage of real time experienced by the players and the gamemaster. RuneQuest uses the following terms to define time:

- **Real Time:** When the players speak in character, or otherwise describe the "here and now" of the game from their adventurer's perspective.
- **Narrative Time:** The quick passage of time that moves the game along, passing at whatever rate the gamemaster says. Generally used when nothing important is happening.
- **Full Turn:** A full turn represents 5 minutes or 25 melee rounds. It describes a period longer than a melee round. Few combats outside of actual battle last a full turn.
- **Melee Round:** About 12 seconds long, this is the basic unit of time used in combat. One complete round of attacks, parries, spells, and movements happens during a melee round.
- **Strike Rank:** Each melee round consists of 12 strike ranks (SR), measures of how quickly actions can be attempted.
- **Skill Time:** The use of abilities can also mark the passage of time. Though combat skills can be repeated melee round after melee round, a may take much longer. See the *Skill Time* sidebar on page 11 for examples.

STRIKE RANKS

In combat, someone will have the edge—the opportunity to strike first and set the pattern for the combat. **Strike rank (SR)** determines who gets the first chance to make a successful attack, and is based on SIZ, DEX, weapon length, magic points being spent, and can be modified by surprise and movement. A parry does not take any strike ranks.

Each attack of whatever type is attempted in strike rank order, lowest to highest. The character/monster with the lowest total strike rank always attacks first. Strike ranks determine which attacks are resolved first in the melee round, and do not represent each second of that melee round. They have been worked out for the adventurers and creatures encountered in *The Broken Tower*.

The following strike rank modifiers are applied to the listed strike ranks, when applicable.

STRIKE RANK MODIFIERS

Activity	SR
Preparing a new spell or weapon	5
Preparing a weapon, spell or missile	5
Surprised by foe(s) within 3 meters	3
Surprised by foe(s) within 4–9 meters	1
Movement: each 3 meters	+1
Magic points used: 1 point	0
Magic/Rune points used: each +1 point	+1

MAGICAL ATTACKS AND STRIKE RANK

To determine the strike rank for spirit magic spells, add the strike modifier for the magic points used in the spell to the adventurer's DEX strike rank modifier. Remember that the first magic point used in the spell has no strike rank modifier. Any subsequent spells require 5 strike ranks to prepare, even if the same spell is being used.

Most spirit magic spells need at least one hand free. Because of this, 5 additional strike ranks must be added to an adventurer's normal strike rank for a spell if they are switching from a weapon to the use of a spell in that melee round. This requirement does not apply to Rune spells.

However, casting a spell such as Bladesharp or Fireblade on a weapon held in the hand only involves adding the normal strike rank for casting the spell to the normal strike rank for that weapon for that melee round.

Sorala, Daughter of Toria

Rune magic spells always take effect at strike rank 1. If more than 1 magic point is used to boost a Rune magic spell, or otherwise increase its effects, 1 strike rank is added for each additional magical point after the first.

Spirit and Rune spells are described on pages 19 and 22-24.

STRIKE RANK LIMITS PER MELEE TURN

No action or combination of actions may be performed in one melee round if the total strike rank necessary adds up to more than 12. If an action requires more than 12 strike ranks (including strike ranks for magic points spent, DEX strike rank, unprepared spell, and any boosting magic points), more than one melee round is needed to cast the spell. A spell requiring 37 strike ranks will take 3 full melee rounds to cast and takes effect on strike rank 1 of the fourth melee round.

MULTIPLE ACTIVITIES OUTSIDE OF MELEE

An adventurer not involved in melee can conceivably do many things in one round, always keeping in mind that there are only 12 strike ranks to work with.

For example, an adventurer with DEX 11 (with a DEX strike rank of 3) could cast a Disruption spell, taking 3 strike ranks. They could then move 9 meters (3 more strike ranks) and take out their bow and arrow (5 strike ranks for readying a weapon). The adventurer is then stuck because firing the arrow would take another 3 strike ranks and there is only 1 strike rank left in the melee round. At the gamemaster's discretion, the 5 strike ranks it took to ready the bow and arrow could have been combined with the 3 strike ranks of movement. This would give the adventurer the time necessary to loose an arrow. Note that an adventurer with average DEX could loose two arrows in one melee round (strike rank 3 for the first arrow, then 5 to ready a new arrow and then 3 for shooting the new arrow, for a total of 11).

In short, each strike rank is considered separately when outside of direct melee contact with a foe.

MULTIPLE ACTIVITIES WITHIN MELEE

When engaged in melee, the adventurer must spend their time attacking and defending. While an adventurer might throw a spell at an oncoming foe and then engage that foe in combat within the same round, **an adventurer cannot, while engaged in combat, attack both physically and magically.** An adventurer that starts a round engaged in melee may either attack and defend normally or defend normally and attack magically, but not both.

An adventurer's strike rank indicates when they may initiate an attack. However, the adventurer is considered to be performing that attack for the entire round and can do little else except parry or dodge.

MOVEMENT

Movement is rated in flexible units, called **Move (MOV)**. Each point of MOV is usually considered to be 1 meter in combat, much more when not in combat. An unencumbered adventurer not engaged in melee combat may move 8 movement units in a melee round, or 24 meters. For each unit (3 meters) of movement an unengaged adventurer makes during the melee round, add 1 to their strike rank if they wish to take any action. An adventurer engaged in melee cannot move until disengaged.

TRAVEL TIME

The amount of time it takes to go from one place to another depends on how hard the route traveled is and whether the travelers are mounted, on foot, or with wagon. A group can only go as fast as its slowest member. In *The Broken Tower*, the most relevant amount travel speed is roughly 2 km/hour when mounted, or 1 km/hour on foot, based on the adventurer's travel speeds and the weather at the time of the adventure.

RUNES

Runes are intrinsic to Glorantha, the cosmic powers that define the world and are manifested by the gods. Known from the earliest prehistory, the Runes suffuse everything in and about the world. They are the building blocks of Glorantha, symbols, archetypes, embodiments, and actual matter or energy of the Middle World. Runes originated with the very creation of Glorantha; they define the cosmos and everything in it. The earliest gods are associated with Runes, and philosophers hold that the gods themselves may merely be personifications of the Runes.

Whatever their nature, Runes are symbols with latent power. People mark their possessions and even their own bodies with Runes. They not only characterize reality, but are used to manipulate the world. Merely looking at or writing a Rune isn't enough: these powers can only be unlocked with extensive training and preparation, such as being a shaman or priest.

TYPES OF RUNES

There are four types of Runes: **Elements**, **Powers**, **Forms**, and **Conditions** (though the latter are not discussed in this quickstart). Each Rune has different associations, from elements, behaviors, attitudes, skill categories, weapons, sensations, creatures, and even physical phenomena. Runes are rated like other abilities, with a percentage value indicating how strong an affinity the adventurer has with the Rune. The higher the Rune's rating, the more strongly its influence should guide the adventurer and their actions.

Each Power and Form Rune is directly opposed to another Rune. The rating in one Rune is balanced against its opposite, with the two values equaling 100%. If one Rune's value increases, the other decreases.

USING RUNES

The Runes are used for magic, to augment certain skills with Runic inspiration, and to define personality.

RUNE MAGIC

Each Rune spell is associated with one or more Runes. The chance of casting a cult Rune spell is equal to the caster's rating in that Rune. If more than one Rune rating applies, the player chooses which Rune to use. See page 20 for more on Rune magic.

RUNIC INSPIRATION

Runes may be used as inspiration to augment skills or increase the chance of success on a resistance roll. What can be augmented depends on the specific Rune: an Elemental Rune may be used to augment a single non-combat skill within its skills category, with a sense associated with the Rune, or with an elemental weapon, and a Power or Form Rune may be used by character to augment any skill being used in accordance with that Rune.

To be inspired by a Rune, the player must suggest and request an appropriate augment to a skill, with the gamemaster's approval. If the adventurer has already rolled to be inspired by a Rune or passion during the situation at hand, they cannot try to be inspired by either the same or a different Rune or passion. Additionally, the bonus from inspiration cannot be combined with an augment from another skill.

The duration is almost always the duration of a combat or battle, or an appropriate amount of time determined by the gamemaster.

The player must roll against the Rune's percentile rating on a D100:

- **Critical Success:** Add +50% to the chosen ability.
- **Special Success:** Add +30% to the chosen ability.
- **Success:** Add +20% to the skill being augmented.
- **Failure:** Subtract –10% from all rolls using that Rune until a day is spent meditating on the Rune.
- **Fumble:** Immediately lose –1D10% from the Rune and become overcome by psychic turmoil. This turmoil might last for a few minutes or a few days, determined by the gamemaster. During that time, the character cannot use that Rune at all (including Rune magic based on that Rune), and must even avoid acting in accordance with the Rune. A Rune cannot be reduced to less than 0%.

RUNES AND PERSONALITY

Runes are universally archetypes, manifest in the cosmos and in the psyche. As a result, they influence feelings and tendencies; an adventurer strongly affiliated with a Rune acts in accordance

Name	Type	Symbol	Associations	Gods	Opposes
Darkness	Element	●	Darkness, Stealth skills, Listen, secrets, cold, hunger, blunt weapons, insects.	—	—
Water	Element	≋	Water, Agility skills, Taste, blood, mercurial, nets and whips, fish.	—	—
Earth	Element	□	Earth, Communication skills, Search, worldly, pragmatism, sensual, axes, reptiles.	Ernalda	—
Fire/Sky	Element	☉	Fire, sky, sun, Perception skills, Scan, purity, chastity, idealism, spears and bows, birds.	—	—
Air	Element	ᚷ	Air, storm, Manipulation skills, Smell, violence, pride, unpredictability, swords, mammals.	Orlanth	—
Moon	Element	◐	Moon, spiritual liberation, Magic skills, balance, time, curved weapons.	Seven Mothers	—
Harmony	Power	III	Harmony, compromise, generosity, peace, compassion, community.	Ernalda, Issaries	Disorder
Disorder	Power	Ⴆ	Disorder, egocentric, greed, strife, thoughtless, self.	—	Harmony
Stasis	Power	⌒	Stasis, unchanging, resolute, determination, obstinate, inert.	—	Movement
Movement	Power	ຈ	Movement, change, impulsive, rebellious, reckless, energetic.	Orlanth, Issaries	Stasis
Truth	Power	Y	Truth, knowledge, objectivity, the written text.	Lhankor Mhy	Illusion
Illusion	Power	∴	Illusion, imagination, subjectivity, poetry, art.	—	Truth
Fertility	Power	Ⴟ	Fertility, life, sex, birth, giving, pleasure.	Ernalda	Death
Death	Power	†	Death, separation, ascetic, endings, denial, ruthless.	—	Fertility
Man	Form	⚐	Mankind, civilization, settled, sociability, ethics.	Daka Fal	Beast
Beast	Form	▽	Animal-kind, savage, wild, untamed, instinctive.	—	Man
Chaos	Form	♆	Chaos, evil, annihilation, perversion of the other runes.	—	—

with that Rune. When the opportunity arises to behave one way or another, an adventurer's Runes can either be used as casual guidelines or may be used by the gamemaster.

- **Casual Use of Runes:** Players sometimes do not know what their adventurers would do under special circumstances. At these times, the player should roll a D100 to determine behavior and consult a suitable Rune. If the result is less than the Rune, the adventurer will follow that Rune's guidance. If the number is larger, the adventurer will do the opposite (especially for opposing Runes).
- **Magical Tests:** Sometimes adventurers must pass magical tests, either by simply having a Rune affinity at a certain value or higher, or rolling against that Rune to demonstrate allegiance to it.

- **Conflicting Runes:** When a dramatic situation emerges where the adventurer's mind is split on a course of action, the gamemaster may call for an opposed roll, using the Rune and its opposite. The winning roll indicates the adventurer's choice, but does not dictate their action: the player can always choose to disobey the adventurer's values or inclinations.
- **Runes and Passions:** An adventurer's Runes may come into conflict with their passions, resolved in the same manner as *Conflicting Runes* (above).

Players should be aware of an impending Rune-driven personality test. They can have their adventurers avoid conflict, but not after the gamemaster initiates the challenge.

PASSIONS

Strong emotions—whether devotion, loyalty, love, hatred, or honor—elevate mere adventures into the stuff of legend. Glorantha myths and history are full of intense emotion, resulting in the heights of heroism and the depths of tragedy. Passionate people may perform with superhuman effort and a greater likelihood of success, and passions provide a means by which this can be done.

Passions are rated just like skills or Runes, with a percentage value indicating how intense the passion is: the higher the more intensely the passion should define the adventurer and their actions.

BASIC PASSIONS

These are the most common passions adventurers possess:

- **Devotion:** A personal and emotional dedication to a specific deity. One can be a good cult member and not be very devoted, but devotion gives an advantage.
- **Loyalty:** The cornerstone of society, including loyalty to one's clan or tribe, or to an individual or temple
- **Love:** An emotional bonding or attraction felt for another individual or for a small group, such as your immediate family.
- **Hate:** Hatred of a clan, tribe, individual, city, nation, or a species.
- **Honor:** Adherence to the martial code of dignity, integrity, and pride. It encompasses correct behavior in warfare and combat, respect of one's peers, and demands respect by others.

USING PASSIONS

Passions define an adventurer's beliefs, inspire them, and can be used to augment abilities. The gamemaster may call for a passion roll, or the player may suggest one. Remember that the gamemaster has the final word on the appropriateness of attempting to use a passion for inspiration. Players are warned that passion rolls can be extremely risky as well as rewarding; a fumbled passion roll results in despair!

INSPIRATION

An adventurer may attempt to become inspired by a passion to augment a skill, with the gamemaster's approval. Only one attempt at inspiration can be made in a situation—such as a combat, battle, meeting, ritual, etc. The inspiration lasts for the time it takes to complete the activity, such as the duration of the combat or battle (with a maximum of one day). The gamemaster determines the actual duration.

Once an attempt is made to be inspired by a Rune or passion during the situation at hand, the adventurer cannot try to be inspired again, even by a different Rune or passion. Additionally, augmentation bonuses from inspiration cannot be combined with an augment from another skill (see page 2).

When attempting to become inspired by a passion, roll against the passion's rating on a D100:

- **Critical Success:** One ability of the player's choice temporarily receives a +50% bonus.
- **Special Success:** One ability of the player's choice temporarily receives a +30% bonus.
- **Success:** One ability of the player's choice temporarily receives a +20% bonus.
- **Failure:** Subtract –10% from all further rolls made for the duration of the situation that brought on the state.
- **Fumble:** The adventurer immediately loses –1D10% from the passion, and is overcome with despair, incapable of doing anything more than running away or hiding. Despair might last for a few minutes or a few days, as determined by the gamemaster. A passion reduced to 0% is removed from the adventurer sheet. A passion cannot go negative in value.

GAINING A PASSION

Passions may be gained during play. Plenty of opportunities are be given to gain enemies, lovers, and loyalties. When something significant occurs to an adventurer, the gamemaster or player may suggest that a passion has been generated. Once in agreement, they then determine the starting value, usually at least 60%.

GLORANTHAN GODS AND CULTS

The following Gloranthan cults appear in *The Broken Tower*, a few of many:

Orlanth, the Storm God (ᚻᚷᚷᚹ) – Orlanth is the King of the Gods, Master of Storms, Death Wielder, and Bringer of Light. He is one of the Seven Lightbringers, and is the chief of those deities. He is the god of warriors, farmers, and rulers. He has two subcults: Orlanth Adventurous is one of them.

Daka Fal, Judge of the Dead (ᚴᚴᚴ) –The cult of Daka Fal supports the reality of human mortality by worshiping the Judge of the Dead, and by drawing upon the dead for strength to survive in life.

Ernalda, Earth Mother and Queen (ᚷᛁᛁᛁᛁ) – Ernalda is the bountiful mother of life, the source of all sustenance. Plants and animals, both wild and domestic, are her children. She is the goddess of women, sex, community, and all the things that live on and in the Earth.

Issaries, God of Communication and Trade (ᚴᛁᛁᛁ) – Issaries is the god of communication, roads, and trade, and is one of the Seven Lightbringers. His worshipers are merchants, traders, caravaners, travelers, and heralds.

Lhankor Mhy, Lord of Knowledge (ᚤᚨ) – Lhankor Mhy is the Lord of Knowledge. He is one of the Lightbringers, and during that epic quest he inherited, found, fought for, and stole many pieces of the old powers.

SKILLS

A skill is an ability representing innate aptitude, training, and experience. While an adventurer can automatically perform routine actions without needing to roll, the gamemaster will call for skill rolls in stressful situations to see if the adventurer or other character is successful.

If the adventurer would always immediately know if they were successful in their skill use, the player should roll. A failed Climb roll to climb a mountain, for example, means the adventurer does not climb the mountain. Likewise, the player should always make combat attacks and parries.

Sometimes the gamemaster, not the player, should make the roll for the adventurer's success. If the adventurer wants to make a Listen roll to see if something is lurking around the next corner, the gamemaster should roll the dice. The player should not know whether the adventurer heard nothing because there was nothing there, or because they failed their roll. As a general rule, though, the gamemaster should let players roll the dice as much as possible.

The gamemaster may declare that a skill roll for an adventurer must be modified because of a particular situation. Since the success percentage for a skill is that for "normal" stressful situations, the changes are generally subtracted from the percentage ability.

SKILLS

Each skill is arranged by skill category and contains the following information:

Skill Name: The name of the skill. Some skills have a narrow specialty, such as Craft (Specific Craft), (Elder Race) Lore or (Homeland) Lore.

Base Chance: The chance characters have when performing the skill for the first time, regardless of culture. Skill category modifiers have been determined for the adventurers in *The Broken Tower* and are already figured into their skills. If the skill is not listed on the adventurer sheet, add the skill category bonus to the base chance.

Description: Abbreviated versions of what can be accomplished using the skill. If in doubt, the gamemaster should determine the scope of any particular skill. Not all RuneQuest skills are presented here.

SKILL TIME

The typical time required to perform a skill is listed below.

A few seconds to one combat round: Weapon attacks, Dodge, First Aid (to stop bleeding), Hide, Jump, Listen, Lore, Spirit Combat, Spirit Dance, Scan.

1–5 minutes: Act, Bargain, Climb, Customs, Conceal, Dance, Fast Talk, First Aid (to heal damage), Insight, Intimidate, Lore, Listen, Move Quietly, Play Instrument, Read/Write, Sing, Sleight, Speak, Spirit Lore, Swim, Treat Disease, Treat Poison.

5–30 minutes: Act, Charm, Customs, Dance, Herd, Intrigue, Lore, Oratory, Peaceful Cut, Read/Write, Search, Sing, Speak, Spirit Travel.

30–60 minutes: Battle, Charm, Customs, Herd, Lore, Oratory, Read/Write, Track.

1 hour to many days: Battle, Charm, Farm, Herd, Lore, Manage Household, Meditate, Prepare Corpse, Read/Write, Survival, Worship.

AGILITY SKILLS

- **Climb (40):** Climbing up or down walls, trees, cliffs, or any other surface.
- **Dodge (DEX×2):** Avoiding being hit by an attack. See *Dodging* on page 14.
- **Jump (DEX×3):** Leaping for height or distance over obstacles, as well as falling (or landing) well.
- **Ride (type) (05):** Riding a horse or other riding animal. See *Mounted Combat* on page 16 for more information.
- **Swim (15):** Staying afloat and moving in a desired direction while in the water.

COMMUNICATION SKILLS

- **Act (05):** Portraying a different persona, whether in a staged performance or in a social situation
- **Art (05):** The creation of images or objects such as painting and sculpture.

MANDATORY RUNE AND PASSION ROLLS

Runes and passions with a rating of 80% or more place the adventurer at the mercy of the gamemaster. Such extreme passions require mandatory rolls whenever the gamemaster chooses. In general, the gamemaster has two options if the player has the adventurer do something inappropriate for the rating in the Rune or passion.

Opposed Rolls: Ask the player they would like to make an opposed roll with the Rune or passion against another Rune or passion. If the opposed ability wins the contest with the Rune or passion trait, the adventurer can act in a different manner, as dictated by the ability that won.

Reduce the Rune: Immediately reduce the Rune or passion to some level below 80%.

- **Bargain (05):** Negotiation and compromise, haggling: used when buying and selling.
- **Charm (15):** Physical attraction, seduction, flattery, or simply warmth of personality, used to compel a desired reaction.
- **Dance (10):** Performing a social, ceremonial, erotic, martial, or sacred dance.
- **Disguise (05):** Creating a convincing disguise using appropriate materials (costumes, cosmetics, wigs, or hairpieces).
- **Fast Talk (05):** Convincing one or more people to agree with whatever the fast talker is saying, deceiving them into thinking that the user is logically correct
- **Intimidate (15):** Frightening or compelling a person to act in a certain way.
- **Intrigue (05):** Knowing what is going on at a court, great temple, warlord's camp, bureaucracy, or similar institution.
- **Orate (10):** Speech used to make groups of reluctant listeners take action or grant a request, driven by emotion.
- **Sing (10):** Knowledge of poetry as well as singing or reciting poetry, used in religious rituals as well as a way of remembering oral history, genealogy, and law.
- **Speak Own Language (50):** Speaking one's native language. No roll required when speaking to other natives, generally only used when eavesdropping, translating, or in difficult circumstances.
- **Speak Other Language (00):** Speaking another language. Languages mentioned in *The Broken Tower* are Esrolian, Heortling, Tarshite, New Pelorian, Praxian, Theyalan, and Tradetalk (a common tongue). Magical languages include Auld Wyrmish (spoken by dragons and their kind), Earthtongue (earth elementals and associated beings), Spiritspeech (spirits), and Stormspeech (creatures of air and storm).

KNOWLEDGE SKILLS
- **Battle (10):** Leading warriors and surviving in massed combat.
- **Customs (type) (own 25 | other 00):** Knowing the behavior, etiquette, law, traditions, and community standards of a group.
- **Evaluate (05):** Estimating the worth of artifacts and goods and valuable natural materials.
- **Farm (05):** Plowing, planting, growing, and harvesting crops, and caring for common domestic animals.
- **First Aid (10):** Treating injuries or victims in shock. See page 18 for more on First Aid and injury.
- **Herd (type) (05):** Keeping individual animals together in a herd, maintain the herd, and moving the herd from place to place.
- **Lore (type) (variable):** Each lore is a specialized body of knowledge, such as Animal Lore (05), Celestial Lore (05), (Cult) Lore (05), Draconic Lore (00), (Elder Race) Lore (05), (Homeland) Lore (own 30 | others 00), Mineral Lore (05), and Plant Lore (05).
- **Manage Household (10):** Handling the property and resources (property, followers, agents, and slaves) of a farm, herd, market, workshop, temple, or palace.
- **Read/Write (type) (00):** Reading and writing in a script. *The Broken Tower* mentions the following written languages: Theyalan, New Pelorian, and Auld Wyrmish.
- **Survival (15):** Surviving in a rural or wilderness environment, including foraging, building a fire, and finding shelter.

MAGIC SKILLS
Skills relating to the Spirit World are discussed in *The Spirit World* (page 19).

- **Meditate (00):** Entering a trance-like state to achieve inner calm and to restore serenity and focus. Meditate can augment spells and skills, and meditating can help restore spent magic points (see page 20).
- **Prepare Corpse (10):** Properly laying out a corpse, preparing it for the final rites and knowing traditional death rituals or spells.
- **Spirit Combat (20):** Battling a hostile spirit (see page 19).
- **Worship (deity) (05):** Linked to a specific god, this takes a full day to perform and must be held on sacred ground.

MANIPULATION SKILLS
- **Conceal (05):** Concealed an object so that it may be found only with a Search skill roll.
- **Craft (type) (10):** Making items out of metal, wood, stone, hides, wool, cotton, clay, etc. Specialties include: Brewing, Carpentry, Jewelry, Leatherworking, Masonry, Pottery, Redsmithing, Vinification, and Weaving.
- **Melee Weapon (type) (variable):** Using a specific melee weapon, described in *Combat* (page 13).
- **Missile Weapon (type) (variable):** Using a specific missile weapon, described in *Combat* (page 14).
- **Shield (type) (15):** Using a specific type of shield, described in *Combat* (page 14).
- **Sleight (05):** Using speed or misdirection to manipulate a small object while being watched by others.

PERCEPTION SKILLS
- **Insight (species) (own 20 | other 00):** Evaluating someone's character, emotional state, trustworthiness, and motives based on body language, speech patterns, and other factors.
- **Listen (25):** Listening intently for sound where one would not normally hear it and picking up incidental sounds.
- **Scan (25):** Observing an area for any signs of movement.
- **Search (25):** Scrutinizing an area to find a concealed or lost object or person.
- **Track (05):** Following the trail left by a living being through wilderness and rural areas.

STEALTH SKILLS
- **Hide (10):** Using available cover, including shadows, misty areas, etc., to hide from others.
- **Move Quietly (10):** Moving in silence, without alerting a foe.

COMBAT

Many conflicts descend—or elevate, depending on one's point of view—into combat. Glorantha provides plenty of opportunities for combat, whether formal challenges between groups or individuals, skirmishes between small groups, or full-scale battles between tens, hundreds, and even thousands of combatants.

Combat can be brutal and confusing, increasingly so the more parties are involved. Combatants press together and withdraw, sidestep and maneuver for positions from which to strike or avoid harm. Attackers and defenders move back and forth on uncertain footing, made more perilous by the bodies of the fallen. Visibility might be limited by helmets, and armor often causes loss of mobility and grace. Every moment brings desperate recalculations based on the flow of combat, each loss and victory causing an instant reassessment about whether—or how—to act. Some hesitate, while others act decisively.

The main kinds of weapons used are melee and missile. These weapons differ in concept: melee weapons can be used to parry as well as attack, while missile weapons are normally used only beyond weapon-length range and are unsuitable for parrying.

As a note, these quickstart rules present a streamlined, simpler version of the RUNEQUEST combat rules.

COMBAT TERMS

Armor Points: Armor and some magic spells can reduce damage. Armor absorbs an amount of damage equal to the armor points present.

Damage Done: Once armor points and the effects of any parry has been subtracted from points of damage, the remaining damage, if any, is the damage done to the target.

Damage Points: When dice are rolled to determine damage, their total, plus any additions for weapon type or magic, are the damage points.

Strike Rank Modifiers: Individual modifiers based on an adventurer's DEX, SIZ, and weapon length are totaled to determine the strike rank in which a melee weapon can be used. Missile and thrown weapon strike ranks depend only on the adventurer's DEX. Spell strike ranks normally depend on the DEX of the adventurer and the number of magic points powering the spell.

THE MELEE ROUND

As discussed on page 7, the melee round is the primary unit of time for individual and small group combat. A melee round is an intensely chaotic, organic, and highly situational affair, but to keep things organized, all melees are divided into four phases: **Statement of Intent**; **Movement of Unengaged Characters**; **Resolution of Melee, Missiles, and Spells**; and **Bookkeeping**. Although these phases are taken in turn, the action is usually simultaneous.

- **Statement of Intent:** All participants in the melee round declare their actions. These intentions do not need to be precise, but should be clear. Consult the strike ranks to see who goes first, if there's any question.
- **Movement of Unengaged Characters:** Everyone not engaged in melee may move up to their total movement allowance.

Those moving up to half of their usual movement allowance may also participate in melee, cast a spell, etc. Every 3 meters of movement adds 1 to their strike rank.

- **Resolution of Melee, Missiles, and Spells:** Each attack is resolved in strike rank order, lowest first. The defender may try to parry or dodge the attack. The effects of damage from missiles, spells, or melee weapons take place immediately, unless otherwise indicated. If one opponent disables another before the other can attack, the victim gets no attack at all, whether with missile, spell, or melee weapon. If both have the same strike rank, their DEX characteristics are compared and the fastest combatant strikes first. If DEXs are the same, then the strikes are simultaneous, and damage is not taken until both attacks have been rolled and all damage assessed.
- **Bookkeeping:** After all attacks are resolved, record all changes in status such as magic points spent, damage taken, Healing done, etc.

Once a melee round has been resolved and all phases are complete, play continues with the next melee round, until the combat is resolved one way or another.

QUICK RESOLUTION OF MELEE

The attacker rolls D100 to see if they succeeded in attacking and then a D20 for hit location. If the defender attempts to parry, they roll D100 to see if they succeeded.
One of the following four conditions occurs:

1. If the attacker succeeds and the defender does not, the defender takes damage in the hit location rolled on D20 as above.
2. If the attacker and defender both succeed, the weapon or shield of the defender is affected.
3. If the attacker fails, but the defender successfully parries with a weapon or shield, the attacker's weapon takes damage.
4. If neither succeeds, nothing is damaged.

ATTACKING

A melee (hand-to-hand) weapon or missile (ranged) weapon skill determines the chance of success with an attack. If the player rolls equal to or less than the skill chance on D100, the adventurer has succeeded and managed to hit their opponent. The defender may still manage to avoid damage by parrying or dodging the blow, trusting their armor, or through magic.

Each weapon has a damage rating described as a dice roll. A broadsword, for example, does 1D8+1 damage, which means the user rolls a 1D8 and adds 1 to the result to determine the damage points done. The adventurer may add or subtract a damage modifier, if applicable. Armor and special magic can add or subtract the damage. It is possible that a successful weapon hit does no damage at all, because of the target's armor or some other form of protection, such as magic.

- **Critical Success:** An attack that is not parried or dodged does the weapon's full rollable damage and bypasses any armor the target possesses, even if the armor is natural. If a critical attack is parried, the parrying shield or weapon takes the critical's damage (maximum possible), with any remaining damage going to the defender.
- **Special Success:** An attack that is not parried or dodged allows the attacker to roll damage twice as normal and add the results together. The target's armor reduces the amount of damage, as normal. If a special success is parried successfully, the special success damage (rolled twice and added together) goes to the shield or weapon, with any excess damage going to the defender.
- **Success:** The attack does the normal rolled damage, reduced by the target's armor, as normal.
- **Failure:** A miss.
- **Fumble:** The attacker botched the attack, accidentally throwing their weapon 1D3 meters away.

THE PARRY

A defender armed with a weapon or shield may parry an attack with a relevant weapon or shield skill. If successful, the parry partially or completely blocks the attack. The parry should be rolled whether the attack succeeded or not, for some successful parries can affect a weapon used in an unsuccessful attack. Generally, only a shield can parry ranged attacks, such as arrows or thrown javelins.

With one weapon or shield, an adventurer can attempt to parry one specific attack on any strike rank of the melee round in which the parrying weapon is prepared. An adventurer may attempt to parry additional attacks on subsequent strike ranks at a cumulative –20% penalty for each additional parry.

A parrying weapon can only block damage equal to the parrying weapon's current hit points. If more points of damage get through, those points go on to do damage to a hit location of the defender.

- **Critical Success:** The parrying weapon (and the defender) take no damage. If a critical parry is made against a critical hit, each is treated as a normal successful parry versus a normal successful attack. A critical parry versus a special success is treated as a special parry versus a normal successful attack.
- **Special Success:** The attack is parried and the parrying shield or weapon takes no damage, nor does the defender. If the attack was a critical hit, it is treated as a special success. If the attack was a special success, it is treated as a normal success.
- **Success:** The attack is parried, but the parrying shield or weapon loses 1 hit point. If the attack is a failure, the parrying weapon or shield does its full damage against the attacking weapon, breaking it if damage exceeds its weapon's current hit points.
- **Failure:** The parry fails and the attack either succeeds or fails, based on the attacker's roll.
- **Fumble:** The defender has accidentally thrown their weapon or shield 1D3 meters away.

SHIELDS

Shields can be used to parry or attack. A shield may not be ready for use when the character is using a two-handed weapon or any projectile weapon other than the sling.

When a shield successfully parries a successful attack, the shield loses 1 hit point and the damage of the attack is absorbed entirely. If the attack is a special success and the parry is successful, the shield takes the damage of the special success (rolled twice and added together). If the shield is reduced to 0 hit points, it is entirely broken apart and useless, beyond repair. If the damage of an attack exceeds the shield's hit points, the rest is passed onto the defender (usually their shield arm).

When used against missile weapons, a small shield protects only the shield arm, a medium shield protects the shield arm and one other hit location (player's choice), and a large shield protects the shield arm and two other hit locations contiguous with each other.

When attacking with a shield, the attacker gives up all chance of parrying that round with the shield. The chance to attack is identical to that for parrying.

DODGING

The Dodge skill may be used to avoid a melee attack instead of a parry. Dodge may be used against all attacks from one source, but must be rolled separately against each attack. A successful Dodge against a normal successful melee attack means that the attack missed. However, a special Dodge roll is necessary against a special success and a critical Dodge is necessary to avoid a critical success. If the Dodge roll is fumbled, then the attacker scores an automatic normal hit, unless their rolled attack is better.

DISENGAGING FROM MELEE

Sometimes, an adventurer may wish to disengage from melee while their opponent wishes to continue. To disengage, there are three options: retreat (spending one melee round to disengage, doing nothing but parrying and Dodging), knockback (see page 15), and fleeing (turning and running, in which the attacker gets one attack against the fleeing character which cannot be parried or Dodged).

RANGE

A melee weapon is meant for close combat, with the combatants no more than a weapon-length apart. On the other hand, missile weapons have different ranges, with medium range is about half again as many meters as the effective range. An adventurer shooting in this range has 1/2 the normal chance of hitting. Long range is between the limit of medium range and twice effective range. An adventurer shooting at long range has 1/4 the normal chance of hitting. Thrown weapons have no effective value beyond 20 meters.

Harmast, Son of Baranthos

SPOT RULES

The following spot rules cover combat and other situations:

- **Aimed Blows:** An attacker can pick a specific hit location to strike by delaying an attack and waiting for an opening. After announcing the desired hit location, the attack is delayed until strike rank 12. The attack skill is halved, plus any other modifiers. If successful, the blow hits where desired. This applies only to melee and missile combat, not with spells.

- **Defenseless or Unaware Opponents:** Add +40% to attacks made against an unaware or immobilized opponent.

- **Falling:** A character takes 1D6 damage for very three meters fallen, applied to a rolled hit location. A successful DEX×5 roll lets the faller specify the hit location they land on. Unlike in combat, any damage in excess of a hit location's hit points are still applied to the falling character. Armor may offer some protection, and Protection and Shield spells will always protect the falling adventurer. The gamemaster may adjust damage based on the relative softness of the surface fallen onto.

- **Fighting while Prone:** An attacker on the ground has half their normal chance performing of successful attack, but parry chance is unmodified. Ignore damage bonuses unless attacking with a natural weapon (fist, kick, claws, etc.). Attacks against a prone character are at +20% to hit.

- **Fighting in the Dark:** Subtract –75% from the skill rating of any skills using visual perception, including attacks, made while in pitch darkness. If the result is negative, the chance of success is 01–05%. A torch or lamp cannot be held in one's shield hand while fighting unless the shield is not used for parrying. The gamemaster may adjust this penalty for partial light.

- **Fire:** A torch is treated as a light club (15%, 1D6, HP 4, SR 5) if used as a weapon. If held to a foe, target takes 1D4 fire damage directly to the specific hit location at the end of the first melee round fire damage. If attempting to ward off the flame (instead of attacking or parrying) the target has a chance of its current POW×5. Protection or Shield spells automatically protect against the flame. If flammable, the target may continue to burn, doing 1D6 damage at the end of each melee round in the affected hit location, with the gamemaster determining the chance of it spreading to another hit location. To douse or smothering a fire, roll the fire damage for each hit location, then 1D6 for the attempt against each hit location affected. The higher roll succeeds. A successful extinguish roll is required for each burning hit location.

- **Grappling:** A successful grapple means the rolled hit location is grabbed. A parry with a weapon means the weapon arm was caught instead, a parry with shield means the shield has been grasped. Defense can be applied against the initial attack with this skill, and a parry with fist or grapple means that the hold was blocked. After a successful attack, the grappler may attempt to immobilize the limb grasped, or throw the foe in the next melee round. To do so they must make another successful grapple attack. Failure means the hold has been broken. To immobilize a limb, the attacker must also succeed in a STR versus STR roll. If this roll is not made, they still have hold of the limb, but it is not immobilized. To throw a foe, an adventurer must make a roll on the resistance table of STR+DEX versus the SIZ+DEX of the foe. Again, failure of this roll means the character did not manage to throw their foe, although the character still maintains a grip. If thrown, an adventurer must make a DEX×5 roll on D100 or suffer 1D6 damage in a random hit location. Armor protects against this damage. If two characters are attempting to wrestle each other, two successful attacks mean they have grasped each other. Two successful immobilizations (one for each) may either mean nothing was accomplished (if they are contradictory) or that both succeeded. Two throws cancel each other. An adventurer's attempt to immobilize should always be rolled before their opponent's attempt to throw. After the initial attack (if it is successful), strike rank should be based on DEX alone, without consideration of SIZ or weapon length.

- **Helpless Opponent:** A totally helpless opponent can be killed with any weapon unless the attacker rolls a 96–00, which is either a failure or a fumble, based on the attacker's skill rating.

- **Knockback:** To knock an opponent down or force them back the attacker must stated this intent the start of a melee round, then make a successful attack with the weapon, shield, or body part intending to knock the target down with. The attacker's STR+SIZ are compared with the defender's SIZ+DEX as a resistance roll (see page 6). If successful, the target is knocked back 1D3 meters. A special success knocks the target down (see *Fighting While Prone*, see page 15). A critical result knocks the target down as well as disarming them. The target does not take any damage from the knockback itself. If the knockback is not successful, the attacker must roll DEX×5 or fall. If successful, the attacker is knocked back 1D3 meters instead. A fumbled attempt at a knockback has the normal fumble penalties. An attempt at a Knockback always happens on strike rank 12. The attacker may not attack in any other way, but may defend and parry normally during this round.

- **Shooting at Protected Targets:** The chance of hitting a foe behind some form of protection, such as an arrow slit in a wall, is the same as normal. However, if the hit location rolled is not visible to the archer, the arrow or other missile hit the protection, not the target. A critical hit hits in any case. Reroll the hit location until it matches an exposed area. The above applies also to melee combat over barriers, fences, castle walls, etc.

- **Shooting at Moving Targets:** Movement of a target directly toward or away from the archer (a general term meaning any user of a missile weapon) has no effect on the probability of hitting it. A target moving at an angle from the archer reduces the archer's chance by half. An evading target reduces the archer's probability by half. An evading character may only move half their normal movement and may do nothing else but move and evade. These effects are cumulative.

- **Shooting into Melee:** An attacker shooting into a crowded melee may hit an ally. In these cases, divide the attacker's skill rating by the number of combatants in the melee. If the reduced chance is a success, the attack hits the intended target. If the roll is higher than the reduced roll but lower or equal to than the normal skill rating, the attack hits another combatant (the gamemaster should determine randomly).

- **Shooting While Moving:** An adventurer cannot shoot while moving or dodging. The only exception to this is mounted archery (see *Mounted Combat*, page 16).
- **Thrown or Dropped Objects:** A palm-sized object balanced for throwing may be thrown 1 meter for every STR point the adventurer has that exceeds its SIZ. If the thrown object is unbalanced or awkward, the distance it can be thrown falls off to 1 meter for every extra 3 STR powering the throw. Roll DEX×5 to hit a target with a casual object, doing 1D3 damage, plus half the thrower's damage bonus. For throws over 10 meters, subtract −3% for every meter in excess of 10 meters. For every 3 kilograms an object weighs, add 1D8 to the damage it does (round down). An object can be effectively thrown by an adventurer if it weighs no more kilograms than the character has STR points. Use the *Falling* rules (above). The damage from the falling object is the same, with any necessary alteration depending on the size of the object dropped. A large object hits 1D6 locations at once, doing the same damage to each, causing more total damage. If the object is flung downward, the half damage bonus is added. The weight of the object has little to do with the damage in this case.
- **Two Weapon Use:** Should a character wish to wield a weapon in each hand, they can be used for two attacks, two parries, or one attack and one parry. Unless trained specifically, use of the weapon in the "off" hand is at 1/2 the normal skill rating. The second attack is made at a strike rank equal to the strike rank of the first attack added to the usual strike rank for the second weapon. If both strike ranks add up to more than 12, then both cannot attack in one round.

MOUNTED COMBAT

An adventurer can fight with weapons or use magic, while mounted on a riding animal, though all skill rankings are equal to the lower of the ability or the Ride skill. It is not possible to use a two-handed swinging weapon while mounted.

The two most useful tactics in mounted combat are: **the charge** (usually with a lance), which requires at least 20 meters of space, and uses the damage bonus of the mount instead of the rider; and **mounted archery**, which has no penalty, but is limited to simple missile weapons.

Unless a riding animal is a trained for combat, it will not fight in a battle. When riding an untrained mount, the rider must make a Ride skill roll every melee round and any time the animal is damaged. If the roll is unsuccessful, the character must spend the next melee round calming the mount using another Ride roll, to the exclusion of all else. If the roll fails or the rider does not try, the animal will bolt away from the excitement.

A trained mount will fight for itself and the rider need only sit on the animal. Ride rolls are not necessary and active spells can be cast. A mounted combatant striking downward with a one-handed weapon effectively hits only the top half of the target. Roll D10+10 for hit location instead of a D20. For combatants on foot striking up with a one-handed weapon at a mounted target, roll for the hit location but any hit on the opposite side of the rider strikes the mount instead.

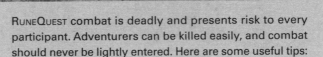

SURVIVING COMBAT

RuneQuest combat is deadly and presents risk to every participant. Adventurers can be killed easily, and combat should never be lightly entered. Here are some useful tips:

Always prepare before a melee. Cast defensive and weapon-enhancing spells before combat if possible.

Missile weapons are deadly. Missile weapons are useful against foes, as they cannot be parried; only blocked by a shield (if the target was prepared for the attack). This goes both ways!

Armor saves lives. Even light armor can greatly increase the chance of survival. Defensive magic is equally useful. Casting 3 points of the Shield spell is the equivalent of wearing bronze plate!

Magic—especially Rune magic—is a game changer in combat. Whether used offensively or defensively, magic spells can change battlefield conditions and take foes out of combat, and greatly boost one's own capabilities.

Always be willing to run away. If the combat goes poorly, always be willing to sound the retreat and run away!

Almost everyone wants to live. Not every fight need be to the death. Most wild animals flee when wounded, and intelligent foes might surrender. Ransoming a captured foe is inevitably more lucrative than looting a corpse.

ENCUMBRANCE AND MOVEMENT PENALTIES

No adventurer can carry everything. RuneQuest handles Encumbrance—the effect of carrying weight as one moves—through a basic system measuring the weight and bulk of items in "things." For the purpose of these quickstart rules, Encumbrance rules are not used, though the gamemaster may wish to add a suitable penalty (−10% or higher) to all skills relating to movement and physical activity for adventurers that are clearly carrying too much.

DAMAGE

Adventurers can suffer many kinds of injury: cuts and concussions from weapons, burns from fires, falls, etc. This is called damage, and points of damage are subtracted from hit points. Armor protects its wearer by subtracting its value from the amount of damage. The rest of the damage gets through, to be subtracted from the hit points of the hit location struck, as well as the adventurer's overall hit points. Hit points can be restored over time, with magic, or with the First Aid skill, but when a hit locations' hit points are exceeded, or the adventurer is out of hit points, bad things can happen.

It is important to record all damage taken by an adventurer and to keep track of each separate injury!

ARMOR

Armor is the last barrier between an adventurer and an incoming weapon, fang, or claw, absorbing damage and, keeping the wearer intact. Different hit locations may bear different forms of armor. Unlike weapons and shields, the armor points for armor never change, even if a blow exceeds the armor points covering the hit location struck. Its armor points are never reduced through damage.

HIT LOCATIONS

Bodies are organized into areas called hit locations. Humans have seven **hit locations**, all listed on the adventurer sheet. Physical damage usually occurs in a specific hit location; points of damage are subtracted from the hit location as well as from the character's total hit points. To determine hit location, roll D20 and consult the character's hit location table (either on the adventurer sheet or in their writeup).

RESULTS OF DAMAGE

Anyone that has taken enough damage to reduce their total hit points to 0 or less dies at the end of the combat round unless Healed or otherwise brought to positive hit points. The sum of hit points in all hit locations add up to more than the total hit points; meaning that someone can be disabled or killed by many small wounds. A character (adventurer or other) falls unconscious if only 1 or 2 total hit points remain, and dies at the end of the melee round if the total hit points are equal to or less than 0.

An individual hit location can take damage beyond the actual hit points in the location. The severity of the damage has different effects, depending on the hit location:

- **Damage Equals or Exceeds the Hit Location's Hit Points:** Limbs become useless. Anything held in the arm is dropped. If a leg or abdomen, the character calls to the ground. See *Fighting While Prone* on page 15. If the abdomen, a character can continue to fight, but if not healed or treated with First Aid within ten minutes they will bleed to death. If the chest, the character cannot fight and bleeding must be stopped by First Aid, or they will die in 10 minutes. If in the head, the character is unconscious and must be healed or treated with First Aid within five minutes or die.

Vasana, Daughter of Farnan

- **Damage Equals or Exceeds Double Location Hit Points:** A character cannot take more than twice the possible points of damage in an arm or leg from a single blow: the rest have no effect. Further blows to that limb affect the hit points of the character. The character is incapacitated, in shock, and can no longer fight until healed. They may try to heal themselves. If the head, chest, or abdomen receive more than twice as much damage as they have hit points in that location, the adventurer becomes both unconscious and begins to lose 1 hit point per melee round unless healed or treated with First Aid. Successful CON rolls do not stop such hit point loss.

- **Location Equals or Receives Triple Location Hit Points:** A limb hit for three times more points than it can take in a single blow is severed or irrevocably maimed, and the character is also functionally incapacitated. A head, chest, or abdomen hit for three times as much damage as the character has hit points in that location results in instant death.

SEVERED AND MAIMED LIMBS

Only a 6-point Healing spell (or its equivalent, such as Heal Wound stacked with 6 magic points) applied within ten minutes can restore a severed limb, assuming all parts are available. Otherwise, healing magic specifically described as capable of regrowing limbs (such as the Regrow Limb Rune spell) may be used to restore a severed limb. However, any healing magic which restores hit points can cure a maimed limb, if all the hit points are restored within ten minutes. If that time limit is passed, the limb is useless, even though the hit points can be restored. To get the use of the limb back, the adventurer must receive magic capable of regrowing limbs.

DEATH

An adventurer reaching the end of a melee round with 0 hit points is dead. Upon death, the soul separates from the body, to travel through the Underworld to the Court of Silence, the gateway to the afterlife. Once there, the Judge of the Dead determines the soul's fate, and it departs for whatever afterlife it is assigned. Prior to judgment, it is possible to resurrect an adventurer with powerful magic. After judgment, only a heroquest can bring the dead back to life.

HEALING

Damage can be erased by Healing magic, the First Aid skill, or by natural healing.

- **Healing Magic:** A Healing spell can be used any number of times to cure any injury. Thus, if an adventurer has taken a 7-point wound, and uses magic to cure 4 points of damage, they then cure the other 3 points in the next melee round.
- **First Aid:** This skill is used to stop bleeding, restore lost hit points, revive unconscious characters, etc. Use First Aid per injury to a specific hit location for any living creature. It takes one melee round to stop bleeding or dying of their wounds. If unsuccessful, the user may try again in the next round. It takes five full melee rounds of First Aid to heal damage. A successful First Aid roll heals 1D3 damage to an injured location. A special success heals 2D3 damage points, and a critical success heals 1D3+3. One can't heal more points of damage than was taken. A fumbled First Aid causes a further 1D3 damage. An injury that immediately kills an adventurer cannot be treated with First Aid. If anything else is done during the five melee rounds in which the user performs this skill, the recipient loses 2 hit points. First Aid can only be used successfully once against an injury to a specific hit location, but it may be tried again and again until successful.
- **Natural Healing:** All living creatures heal naturally with time. The character's healing rate dictates how many hit points are recovered in each location at the end of each game week. For natural healing, it is the location that matters, not the number of wounds. An adventurer cannot engage in strenuous activity—rest is necessary for healing! As a location recovers lost hit points, the level of injury improves and the speed of healing increases.

I NEED HEALING!

At some point, an adventurer will need healing during or after taking damage. These are the options:

A lot of healing fast: Cast Heal Wound (a common 1-point Rune spell) stacked with as many magic points as can be spared. Or cast Heal Body (a 3-point Rune spell).

A little healing fast: Cast the spirit magic Healing spell. It might not be enough to fix a deadly wound, but it might be enough to restore use of an incapacitated limb. Or drink a healing potion if one is available.

A little healing slowly: Use the First Aid skill. It takes 5 full melee rounds and only heals a small amount of damage but has no magical cost. Each use can fix one specific injury.

You need healing but aren't in a rush: Get some bed rest and let natural healing take care of it.

SPIRIT MAGIC

Spirit magic is the most basic and common magic found in Glorantha. It concerns communication with the spirits that reside in the natural energy currents of the world and is practiced in one form or another by nearly every Gloranthan culture and religion. To cast a spirit magic spell, the caster concentrates their will and alters the spiritual energy currents to create an effect. This done through spending **magic points**. For this reason, spirit magic spells (sometimes called "battle magic") while powerful, are of short duration—usually two minutes—and drain many magic points from the user.

An adventurer has a POW×5 chance of successfully casting a spirit magic spell. If the roll is unsuccessful, no magic points are expended, and the adventurer may try again in the next melee round. If the caster's concentration is broken in any way before they have finished with casting a spell (such as taking damage), they cannot cast the spell and must try again. However, no magic points are lost in the attempt.

All spirit magic spells are either **instant** or **passive**. Once cast, the caster need pay no further attention to them and they continue to work, regardless of what the caster does next.

THE FOCUS

Spirit magic spells require a **focus**, a reminder and token of the spell. Contact with the focus releases the caster's magical energies and makes the spell work. Foci can be tattoos, ritual scars, carvings, trinkets, jewelry, etc. Casting a spirit magic spell without a focus takes two melee rounds, the first round spent in visualization of the spell's focus and its intended target. Runes may even be carved into the intended target of the spell, such as weapon.

MAGIC POINTS

Magic points represent the quantity of life energy that an adventurer can use to cast spells. They are expended when casting spells. Every spell costs a certain number of magic points to cast, but some spells can have additional magic pointed added to overcome a Countermagic or Shield spell. Additional points put into a spell do not count for the spell's effect, but are considered when opposing or overcoming other spells.

An adventurer with 0 magic points falls unconscious until their magic points return to a positive value. Magic points are normally regained at the rate of 1/4 the character's total POW every six hours, but can also be regained more rapidly through successful use of the Meditate skill (see below).

RESISTANCE ROLL

All targets, except voluntary ones, resist spells cast at them and need to be overcome (POW against POW) using the resistance table on see page 6. An adventurer may try to augment their chance of success with the resistance roll by using an appropriate spell or through use of the Meditate skill (see, *Meditation* sidebar).

SPIRIT MAGIC SUMMARY

Spell	Cost	Type	Description
Befuddle	2	R, D	Target confused and can only defend until actually attacked.
Bladesharp	Var.	T, D	Adds +5% to hit and +1 damage per point.
Countermagic	Var.	R, D	Blocks 1 point of spirit magic for every point of Countermagic or 1 point of Rune magic per every 2 points of Countermagic.
Demoralize	2	R, D	Target will try to retreat if possible; if not, target attacks at half chance.
Detect Enemies	1	R, I	Points to the closest entity intending harm.
Detect Life	1	R, I	Points to the nearest living creature of SIZ 3 or larger.
Detect Spirit	1	R, I	Points to the nearest disembodied spirit.
Dispel Magic	1	R, I	Cancels 1 point of cast spirit magic per point of Dispel Magic or 1 point of Rune magic per every 2 points of Dispel Magic.
Distraction	1	R, I	Forces targeted spirit to attack the caster instead of anyone else.
Fanaticism	1	R, D	Target increases their chance to hit by half again, but cannot parry. Dodge is halved.
Farsee	Var.	R, D	Each magic point halves the apparent distance as seen by the caster to the rest of the universe.
Glamour	2	T, D	Increases CHA by +8. Increases spirit combat damage by one step, increases all communication and magic skills by +10%.
Heal	Var.	T, I	Each magic point heals 1 hit point in a designated area. Can be used multiple times.
Mobility	1	R, D	Doubles the Movement speed of the target and reduces their strike rank by 1.
Protection	Var.	R, D	Each magic point acts as 1 armor point to the whole body.
Second Sight	3	R, D	Allows the target to view the POW aura of living beings and spirits, and gauge their relative strength.
Slow	1	R, D	Halves the Movement speed of the target and adds 1 to their strike rank.
Spirit Screen	Var.	R, D	Each magic point absorbs 1 point of spiritual damage in spirit combat.
Strength	2	T, D	Increases target's STR by +8, increasing damage bonus by one step (0 to 1D4, 1D4 to 1D6, 1D6 to 2D6) and increasing all Agility and Manipulation skills by +10%.
Visibility	2	S, D	Forces a spirit to take shape in this world and makes it subject to spells. See *Spirit Combat*, below.

Type: T (Touch), R (Ranged), I (Instant), D (Lasts 5 minutes)

SPIRIT COMBAT

Spirit combat plays a huge part of adventuring in Glorantha, but is too complex to fully describe in these quickstart rules. The optional downloadable assistant shaman adventurer includes lengthier rules about the Spirit World and spirit combat, but an abbreviated version is presented here.

Only discorporate beings can initiate spirit combat. Spirit combat is always resolved on strike rank 12 with an opposed Spirit Combat skill roll.

Success means the loser suffers the winner's spirit combat damage, applied to magic points. In a tie, both parties take damage. Special and critical successes are treated the same as with weapons.

Spirit combat ends when one party is reduced to 0 magic points, or flees, using the Spirit Dance skill.

Attacks against spirits from the physical world are resolved on normal strike ranks. Other than spirit combat, only spells and the magical effects laid on weapons magical weapons can harm them, reducing their magic points in place of hit points.

MEDITATION

An adventurer can successfully Meditate uninterrupted for one full hour, attempting no other skill rolls, making any movement, or communicating in any way. No spellcasting may be attempted, and if the gamemaster determines that a distraction might be enough to disturb the Meditation attempt, the adventurer must perform a successful POW×3 roll to resist being distracted from the Meditation attempt. A successful Meditation skill roll yields the adventurer 1 additional magic point, in addition to any restored through normal rest and recuperation. A special success rewards the adventurer with 1D3 and a critical success yields 1D3+1 magic points. If the roll fails, the adventurer recovers no additional magic points, and a fumble causes the loss of 1D3 additional magic points.

SPELL STRIKE RANK

To determine the strike rank when a spell can be cast, total the caster's DEX strike rank plus the magic points of the spell, plus any boosting magic points. The total is the strike rank of the spell.

RANGE

Spirit magic has two ranges: touch (the caster must touch the target) and ranged (50 meters). For touch spells, touching the clothing or armor of the target is usually sufficient unless the spell description declares otherwise.

DURATION

The duration is how long the effects of the spell last, from the strike rank the spell was cast. All temporal spells last five minutes (25 melee rounds). Instant spells cause effects only on the strike rank on which they were cast. Certain spells have permanent effects.

RUNE MAGIC

An initiate of a cult can cast the Rune spells known to that cult. The caster relies on power supplied by that god to cast the spell. When an adventurer casts Rune magic, the caster acts as the deity. The caster imitates the deeds of the deity and thereby evokes the deity's power. The caster always exhibits some form of manifestation of the deity while casting the spell: they might appear to grow larger, burn with an inner glow, crackle lightning from the fingertips, or even start to physically resemble the deity. The more Rune magic cast, the more the deity manifests in the world.

RUNE POINTS

Characters possess Rune points, earned from making permanent sacrifices of POW to their god, enabling access to their cult's Rune magic. Once spent, Rune points must be replenished before they can be used again. They may only be replenished through worship of the deity on a holy day and participation in cult rites.

CASTING RUNE SPELLS

To cast a Rune spell, during the Statement of Intent the player must say what spell is being cast and at which target(s). The adventurer must have sufficient Rune points to cast the spell—the cost of each spell is given in the spell descriptions (following). The caster recites the invocation to the god, either aloud or in the mind, after which the spell takes effect. Rune magic spells always take effect at strike rank 1.

The adventurer must then roll against the Rune affinity of that spell. If the roll succeeds, then the spell takes effect, and the Rune points are spent. If the roll is a critical, the spell costs no Rune points.

If the casting success roll is greater than the Rune affinity, the spell is not cast and the Rune points are not spent. If the adventurer was boosting the spell with additional magic points, they lose 1 magic point. On a fumble, the spell fails and the adventurer loses the Rune points for the spell.

Casting a Rune magic spell prevents an adventurer from casting any other Rune magic or spirit magic spells that round. The sole exceptions are Extension, which is cast at the same time as the spell it is intended to extend, and Illusion spells. For more information, see the description of these Rune spells.

RESISTANCE ROLL

Many spells require the caster overcome the target's POW using a resistance roll (see page 6). An adventurer may try to augment their chance of success with the resistance roll by using an appropriate spell or through meditation (see *Increasing the Casting Chance*, nearby).

BOOSTING A SPELL

A caster may always use additional magic points to boost a spell, regardless of type. This is typically done to overcome a Countermagic or Shield spell, or other magic defenses.

STACKABLE RUNE MAGIC

All Rune magic spells have an initial Rune point cost that allows one casting of the spell. Rune magic spells can be stacked (combining several castings into one) if the spell is described as stackable. This provides a much more powerful effect when the spell is cast. There may be a ceiling to the maximum allowed to be cast together. All of the Rune points are cast at one target, in a single melee round and take effect at strike rank 1.

Vostor, Son of Pyjeem

CHARACTERISTICS OF RUNE SPELLS

Unless the spell description says otherwise, all Rune magic spells are passive with a duration of 15 minutes and a range of 160 meters. A Rune magic spell is always twice as strong as a spirit magic spell of the point cost. Thus, it takes 2 points of Dispel Magic to dispel a 1-point Rune magic spell.

INCREASING THE CASTING CHANCE

There are various means of increasing the chance of casting a spell, whether Rune or spirit magic. The most important are **meditation**, **ritual practices**, and **augmenting with skills**.

- **Meditation:** sole purpose of this meditation is the casting of the spell, and does not yield additional magic points. While meditating, the adventurer can take no other action. If injured, roll INT×3 or the concentration is broken and the character must start over to get the bonus. If the roll is successful, the adventurer gets the bonus.
- **Ritual Practices:** These take on many forms, but allow the caster's spiritual energy to be focused, to increase the chance of success. Although the magician can eat and sleep during while performing the ritual practices, they can do little else. If they take time away from their ritual practices to do something else (adventure, get sick, give birth, etc.), that time is deducted from the actual time spent in ritual. The spell casting is rolled at the completion of the ritual. If the roll succeeds, the spell is cast and any magic points or Rune points used in the spell are spent.
- **Augmenting with Skills:** Skills such as Dance, Sing, Perform, Speak Magical Language, etc. may be used to help improve casting chances, as with other abilities (see *Augmenting Abilities*, page 2). If only 1 melee round is spent performing the skill, the chance of success with the augmenting skill is halved. If the character spends 2 melee rounds performing the skill, the chance of success is normal. As with Meditation (above), distraction can cause the augment to fail.

The following table shows these benefits:

INCREASING SPELLCASTING CHANCE

Bonus	Meditation	Ritual
+5%	1 melee round	—
+10%	2 melee rounds	—
+15%	5 melee rounds	—
+20%	25 melee rounds	—
+25%	50 melee rounds	—
+30%	—	30 minutes
+35%	—	1 hour
+40%	—	5 hours
+45%	—	10 hours
+50%	—	1 day

MAXIMUM GAME FUN

When writing, thinking, and gaming about Glorantha, always ask yourself, "*Now, in this situation what is the most fun?*" and then go with it. That's the principle of **Maximum Game Fun** (MGF). Keep this in mind whenever you apply the rules of RuneQuest to any situation.

ABOUT GLORANTHA AND RUNEQUEST

Glorantha is a mythic heroic fantasy setting created by Greg Stafford beginning in 1966 and first published in the strategy boardgame *White Bear, Red Moon* in 1975, published by Chaosium. It is a world with a deep and rich setting, drawing influence from the Bronze Age and other ancient world cultures and mythologies.

To better bring the world to life, Glorantha became the setting for a roleplaying game, RuneQuest, published in 1978, also from Chaosium. In the five decades since its creation, hundreds of works—games, stories, novels, card games, board games, computer games, etc.—have fleshed out and portrayed the world of Glorantha, firmly establishing it as one of the most popular original game settings ever.

RuneQuest's percentile-based rules system has been used to drive many other wildly-successful games, including *Stormbringer*, *ElfQuest*, *Ringworld*, and most notably *Call of Cthulhu*, itself one of the most popular roleplaying games worldwide. RuneQuest's simple, intuitive system (also called *Basic Roleplaying*) has directly inspired other games, including *HeroQuest* and *King Arthur Pendragon*, and been influential to dozens, if not hundreds more games and their designs.

Over the years, several editions of RuneQuest have appeared (some under other imprints) but this marks a return to Glorantha being inextricably melded with the RuneQuest system. The rules used in this quickstart are a direct evolution from the second and third editions of the rules and should be the most familiar to players of those editions.

Chaosium, Inc. is proud to announce that this version of RuneQuest has been designed in close collaboration with the creator of Glorantha and the original RuneQuest writers and designers, bringing this edition full circle.

RUNE SPELL DESCRIPTIONS

The following Rune spells are provided for the adventurers and characters in this quickstart. Many more exist. Each spell is described in the following fashion:

- **Rune:** The Rune associated with the spell. To cast the spell, roll this Rune's affinity. "Special" means that the spell uses different Runes, depending on what cult it was learned from.
- **Name:** The name of the spell.
- **(God):** The god whose cult the spell was learned from. "Any" means that all cults know the spell.
- **Description:** The spell's effect, potential targets, and other information.
- **Cost:** The number after the spell's description is the Rune points the spell costs to cast. "Var." = variable.
- **Type:** T=Touch, R=Range is 160 meters, I=Instant, D=Lasts 15 minutes, A=Active

Rune	Spell
□	**Absorption (Ernalda)** – Each point absorbs 1 point Rune magic or 2 points spirit magic, converting them into magic points. Var., R, D
Y	**Analyze Magic (Lhankor Mhy)** – Gives a true statement about at least one function of a single magical item, entity, or substance. 1, T, I
□	**Arouse Passion (Ernalda)** – Adds +20% to one of the target's passions, can create a new temporary passion at 20%. Each point stacked adds +20% to the passion. Var. R, D
X	**Charisma (Ernalda)** – Doubles target's CHA and adds +20% to all communication and magic skills. 1, R, D
Y	**Clairvoyance (Lhankor Mhy)** – Lets the caster see any location within 5 km as if they were there. The caster must have previously been to the location. 2, R (5 km), D
Special	**Command Cult Spirit (All)** – Enables the caster to command any of their cult's spirits if they overcome its POW. 2, R, D
♌	**Dark Walk (Orlanth)** – Allows the user to be totally invisible and soundless in darkness and shadow to anyone within range. 1, R, D
Y	**Detect Truth (Lhankor Mhy)** – Allows the caster to tell whether anyone within a five-meter radius of the spell's target site is lying. 1, R, D
Any	**Dismiss Magic (All)** – Each point cancels 2 points of spirit magic or 1 point of Rune magic. Var., R, I
Special	**Dismiss Elemental (Ernalda/earth, Orlanth/air, Seven Mothers/all but air, Waha/earth)** – Dismisses an elemental of the type listed. With 1 Rune point, the caster can try to dismiss a small elemental. With 2 Rune points, the caster can try to dismiss a medium or small elemental. With 3 Rune points, the caster can try to dismiss a large, medium, or small elemental. The caster of the spell must overcome the POW of the elemental for the spell to work. R, I
Any	**Divination (All)** – Allows the caster to ask a simple question of their deity and receive an answer of up to seven words. One hour to cast. 1
⊚	**Earth Shield (Orlanth)** – Gives a shield infinite armor points for the duration. 3, T, D
□	**Earthpower (Ernalda)** – Draw 1 point of POW and 1D8 magic points from the earth. 3, Self, I
Any	**Extension (All)** – Affects the duration of another spell. For 1 point, the other spell lasts an hour. For 2 points, a day. For 3 points it lasts a week. 1, Spec.
Any	**Find Enemy (All)** – Alerts the caster to anyone within range that intends to harm the caster. 1, R, D
⊚♌	**Flight (Orlanth, Issaries)** – Transports one object (including caster) weighing up to SIZ 6 through the air for duration of the spell. Each extra point adds +6 to SIZ. Flying objects have Movement 12. Var., R, D
□X	**Heal Body (Ernalda)** – Heals all a character's damage, regardless of hit location(s). 3, T, I
Any	**Heal Wound (All)** – Heals hit points equal to the magic points spent. 1, T, I

Rune	Spell
□X	**Inviolable (Ernalda)** – Affects any Ernalda or Orlanth cultist within 3 meters of the caster. Cancels Demoralize, Fanaticism, and other emotion-affecting magic on eligible targets. Those affected will become calm and avoid violence if possible. 1, Self, D
Y	**Knowledge (Lhankor Mhy)** – Allows the caster to read the past history of an item. 2, T, D
♌	**Leap (Orlanth)** – Allows the target to jump up to 6 meters high or 6 meters away for the spell's duration. Each additional point adds +6 meters to the distance. 1, R, D
⑤	**Lightning (Orlanth)** – Summons a blast of lightning, doing 1D6 per point cast to a single hit location if the target's POW is overcome. Armor does not protect against the damage. Var., R, I
ⅢⅠ♌	**Lock (Issaries)** – This spell locks a door or other opening with a STR equal to the number of magic points used. Takes an hour to cast, but lasts 8 weeks. 1, Spec.
⓪	**Madness (Seven Mothers)** – If the target's POW is overcome by the caster, the target suffers effects based on the success: *Critical:* Target goes insane for 30 minus POW days. *Special Success:* Target attacks nearest person as if Fanatic for the next 30–POW minutes. *Success:* Victim collapses for 30–POW minutes and cannot be awakened. *Failure/Fumble:* No effect. 2, R, I
⓪	**Mindblast (Seven Mothers)** – Destroys the INT of the target if the caster overcomes the target's POW. Effect lasts a number of days equal to 1/2 the caster's POW (rounded up), and cannot be dispelled. If the caster achieves a special success in overcoming the target's POW the attack also causes 1D6+2 damage to the target's head. Armor does not protect against this damage, though magical protection will. 2, R, I
Y	**Mind Read (Lhankor Mhy)** – Lets the caster read the conscious thoughts of the target without their consent, though the target can tell there is an intruder in their mind. The caster must overcome the target's POW for the spell to operate. 2, R, D
⑤	**Mist Cloud (Orlanth)** – Creates a bubble of natural-looking mist 2 meters in diameter for every Rune point expended with the spell. Visibility within or through the mist is limited to 1 meter. 1, R, D
Any	**Multispell (All)** – Allows the user to combine two spirit magic spells and cast them at once. This spell affects all spells cast by the recipient over the duration: thus every melee round, the recipient can cast two spirit magic spells. 1, R, D
♌	**Passage (Issaries)** – Must be cast with Lock. Each point allows one additional person to pass through or open the enspelled aperture besides the caster. 1, Spec.
♌	**Path Watch (Issaries)** – Must be laid upon a known path or visible road to be traveled on by the caster. Alerts the user to the direction and number (though not type) of all enemies and traps within a 100-meter radius. Lasts as long as the road lasts and as long as the caster stays awake. 2, S, D
Y	**Reconstruction (Lhankor Mhy)** – Causes any 15-minute sequence from the past to replay for the caster's senses, as long as they are in the immediate area in which it took place. The user must state the time and date of the vision. 3, R, D
⓪	**Reflection (Seven Mothers)** – Reflects spells which fail to overcome the POW of the protected being. The next strike rank, the reflected spells attack their caster. The POW of the reflected attack spell are equal to the caster's at the time the spell was originally cast. Each point stacked with this spell reflects 2 points of spirit magic, or 1 point of Rune magic. Reflection does not work if the incoming spell is too powerful. Var., R, D
⓪X	**Regrow Limb (Ernalda, Seven Mothers)** – Regrows a severed or maimed limb. 2, T, I
Ⅲ	**Safe (Issaries)** – Cast upon a container or opening to bar unwanted passage, and must be boosted with magic points. When anyone other than the caster tries to open the secured container or cross a doorway with this spell, they are attacked by the spell's magic points. If the trespasser's POW is overcome, they take 1D6 points of hit point damage and are forced back. Lasts 8 weeks. 2, T, Spec.
⑤†	**Shield (Orlanth, Waha)** – Every point of Shield gives the wearer 2 points of magical armor and 2 points of Countermagic (equivalent to the spirit magic spell, see page 19). The effects are cumulative with Protection or Countermagic. Var., R, D

Rune	Spell
Any	**Soul Sight (All)** – Allows the recipient to see both the POW aura of the living and to magically know the actual current magic points of other things and creatures, including the amount devoted to currently in-effect spells. 1, R, D
III	**Spell Trading (Issaries)** – Allows the caster to trade one use of any Rune magic (except this one!) in exchange for one use of any Rune spell known by another priest of any cult. 2, T, I
Any	**Spirit Block (All)** – Helps protect the recipient from attack by spirits. Each point of this spell acts as spiritual armor and absorbs 2 points of magic point damage in spirit combat. Var., R, D
Special	**Summon Elemental (Ernalda/earth, Orlanth/air, Seven Mothers/all but air, Waha/earth)** – Caster asks the deity to send an elemental of this type. Elementals come in three sizes: small, medium, and large. The elemental's size depends on how many Rune points are stacked with the spell (and is limited by the maximum size of elemental is available to the cult). Once summoned, the elemental serves the summoning character until it is physically destroyed, or 15 minutes have passed, whichever comes first. Var., R, D
⚡	**Teleportation (Orlanth)** –The caster can teleport to any spot that can be seen, either on their own, or through the eyes of an allied spirit. Each additional Rune point enables one extra living thing to be teleported at the same time, provided they are touching the caster. 3, T, I
Y	**Translate (Lhankor Mhy)** –Translates all words touched by the user's index finger at normal reading speed, leaving an impression of the meaning afterwards. 1, T, D
Y	**Truespeak (Lhankor Mhy)** – Compels the target to speak nothing but the truth for the duration, answering all questions in a literal manner. The caster must overcome the target's POW with each question. 2, R,,D
⚡	**Wind Words (Orlanth)** – Causes the wind to bring conversations to the caster's ears, as if standing next to the speaker. 1, R, D

THE BROKEN TOWER

GETTING STARTED

To play this adventure, you, the gamemaster, should hand out the pregenerated character sheets (pages 42–47), assigning them as desired. You should have at least one set of dice as described on page 1, and something to write with. Copies of the spell lists on pages 22–24 are also advised. The map on page 27 is also useful as a handout, but not essential.

INTRODUCING GLORANTHA

If the players are unfamiliar with Glorantha, the gamemaster should read or paraphrase the following text aloud to the players, establishing the tone of the adventure and providing a brief overview of Glorantha and the setting.

Welcome to Glorantha, a mythic place of heroes and gods, where people hold allegiance to tribe, city, and cult, not to abstract alignments or ideologies. Although humanity is the dominant species, their dominance is due only to the quarrelling of the Elder Races, who still rule large parts of the world.

In Glorantha, the gods and goddesses are real, and through their cults they play an important role in most major events. Would-be heroes of the age are known as adventurers, and each is tied to several of the Runes, cosmic powers that define Glorantha and are likewise manifested by the gods. Powerful deities are associated with the Sun, Earth, Air, Water, Darkness, and the Moon, as well as with Death, Life, Change, Stasis, Illusion, Truth, Disorder, and Harmony, and each has its Rune. Adventurers join the cults of their gods, from which they get magic and aid.

Adventurers are participating and active members of society, whether clan, tribe, city, or other community. They have duties, loyalties, and conflicts beyond being mere freebooters, with ties to the world of Glorantha and the Runes as deep as they are profound. As adventurers advance within their cults, they strengthen their connection to the Runes, gaining power and questing towards becoming true Heroes.

One of the most important places in Glorantha is Dragon Pass. Beset by conflict and blessed with opportunity, it is an extremely magical place, the center of many of the world's great myths. Dragon Pass is prophesied to be the site of the great, apocalyptic series of events called the Hero Wars. A recent revolution against the occupying Lunar Empire has left many of the cities of Dragon Pass in ruins. Nobles, cults, and clans vie for power and authority in their wake, and its liberators struggle to rebuild and reclaim that which was lost.

OPENING SCENE

Read the following text aloud to the players:

You've been on the road for a couple of days, riding in pursuit of the thieves that stole a large portion of your tribe's cattle—one of its greatest sources of wealth. In the course of this heinous crime, they slew two of your kin and wounded another: simple herders, not even tribal warriors. Zarah, your clan-chieftain's wife set you—her boldest and most able-bodied allies—to follow, recover the cattle, and exact retribution for the insult.

One of your injured kinsfolk recognized members of the Greydog clan among the raiders, particularly a man named Danakos, an ambitious and bitter Greydog. The raiders' path led in the direction of Lismelder tribal land, specifically to the Greydog's home village.

At this point, it would be useful for the players to introduce their adventurer, if they have not already done so. Each pre-generated adventurer sheet contains a short introduction encapsulating the core information about the adventurer in their own words, and the players should be encouraged to read or paraphrase these, getting into character as much as desired.

Some of the pre-generated adventurer sheets mention prior connections and relationships between the adventurers, and the gamemaster may ask the players to expand on these, letting everyone settle into their roles. Not everyone needs to get along all the time, and friendly rivalries or uncertain loyalties can add roleplaying opportunities galore.

The adventurers are assumed to have food, drink, and adequate supplies for a few days, and any personal effects needed.

THE BADLANDS OF THE STARFIRE RIDGE

The area the adventurers are in is known by both Colymar and Lismelder tribes as "the badlands", located at the southernmost reaches of the Starfire Ridge, a region almost entirely empty of settlements. Rough and rubble-strewn ground and patchy grasses stretch on as far as the eye can see, broken occasionally by low hills, small ragged copses of trees, jagged rocky formations that bear unreadable and mostly-eroded carvings, and small pools of generally stagnant, muddy water. Eventually, the hills blend into the foothills and mountains of the Starfire Range. Half-buried walls and foundations of long-vanished civilizations point at an age the land was more habitable. Old burial mounds, cairns, and dolmen (single-chamber tombs made of stone slabs) dot the land, alone and in clusters, mostly broken open long ago. Standing stones abound, menhir and markers broken and re-carved over the years, but mostly ignored.

Unlike the rich and verdant lands elsewhere in Dragon Pass, held by the various tribes, the badlands can support little life, thousands of acres of useless land, generally left alone. None of the adventurers have been here before. There are plenty of places in Glorantha called badlands: this is another of them.

What the Adventurers Know

The gamemaster should allow the players to ask any relevant questions they might have, answering any obvious questions about common knowledge (provided in the bullet points below), and asking for skill rolls to provide other information, where applicable. It's generally a good idea to only provide info if it's asked for, to avoid overloading the players with detail that might not be important to them.

- Your clan chief is Baranthos son of Estavos (*father of the adventurer Harmast*), and he is away at a trade-time festival at the Sun Dome Temple, along with many other nobles and landowners of your village, along with a protective force of warriors. His wife Zarah is in charge while he is away, and she asked you to do this deed. *If Harmast is among the adventurers, as her son he is beholden to obey her.*
- When the herders did not return with the cattle, Zarah sent a runner. The runner went to the pastures and found the herders lying on the ground in a row, two dead and the last nearly so.
- The injured herder is named Berra. She claims that while watching the herd as they grazed a couple of kilometers from the village, they were ambushed. Her fellow herders (Endach and Datha) were killed, and Berra was left for dead. She recognized Danakos son of Egrost as the one who stuck a spear through her belly, and said that the other Greydogs were surprised at Danakos' actions.
- The Greydog clan is a part of the Lismelder Tribe, longtime rivals to the Colymar Tribe (the adventurers' own tribal affiliation). The Greydogs contest ownership of the Starfire Ridge with the clans of the Colymar Tribe. The Greydogs

WHAT'S GOING ON?

This information is for the gamemaster, and should not be read to the players.

The **Greydog clan**, part of the Lismelder tribe, are bitter rivals to the Colymar tribe (which the adventurers belong or currently have loyalty to). One of the Greydogs is a particularly ambitious warrior named **Danakos Son of Egrost**, a man with longstanding grievances against the Colymar. When the clan chief and nobles among his tribe went to the Sun Dome Temple for a trader-time festival between many of the clans, Danakos decided that this was his chance to steal from the Colymar any cattle that had not been taken to the market. A dominating bully, Danakos quickly convinced a group of his rogues to accompany him on this raid.

The Greydogs crossed the badlands, sneaking into Colymar land, and found the herd and its tenders. His allies had thought they were just there for theft, and became angry when, rather than just tying them up or knocking them out, Danakos murdered the herders. After a brief argument, they took sixty Colymar cattle, as they were already past the point where they could return empty-handed. Unbeknownst to them, one of the herders, Berra, survived her wound.

Bickering and sullen as they made their way home, on their first night of camping with the stolen herd, the Greydogs encountered a mysterious woman, wandering the plains. Unfortunately for these cattle-thieves, this was

no mere woman, but was the spirit projection of **Idrima**, an old demon goddess from the First Age, long interred beneath an old ruin within the adjacent forest. She was once worshipped in these badlands, and her temple lies in ruins nearby. Dotting the landscape are totem-idols to her, though most have worn away and are unrecognizable, many defaced and pushed over by those who came later.

Idrima still slumbered, lost in a torpor that has lasted millennia, but the thunder of the cattle and the promise of so much meat and blood drove her to partial wakefulness. She sent out one of her dream-wefts, a spirit-being spun of ethereal spirit-stuff and housing her consciousness, anchored to her few idols that still dotted the land. She found the Greydog camp and the herd, and enthralled Danakos, binding him to her will.

Danakos was enthralled by Idrima, and sought to deliver and sacrifice the stolen cattle to her. One of his loyalists balked, and he killed her, bullying the others into submission. They broke camp and rode into the ruins, stabling the cattle there, and entered the ancient tomb, led by their possessed kinsman. Their fates were grim.

Aside from Danakos, only one of the Greydogs is still alive, though insane and hiding from her clan-mate. In the meantime, Danakos is readying a ritual to awaken the old demon-goddess, feeding it offerings in the form of a herd of prized Colymar cattle.

likely used the trade-time festival as an opportunity to raid against their distant neighbors, undoubtedly in return for some past offense.

The above is common knowledge. To emphasize how dastardly these events were, the gamemaster might ask if any of the adventurers if they are friendly or even related to any of the herders. Such an outrage might allow an adventurer to invoke their Loyalty (Colymar Tribe) passion to augment a skill during the events to come.

If the adventurers want to know more, the gamemaster should have them roll for suitable skills.

- A successful **Area Lore (Dragon Pass)** roll reveals that the Greydog named Danakos son of Ergost is a troublemaker. A special success reveals that he has hassled members of the Colymar tribe at various festivals, and picked several fights. A critical success causes the adventurer to remember that he had a cousin in the Colymar tribe through marriage, a cousin he killed in a drunken duel. Forced to pay restitution by the Lismelders, his own tribe, Danakos was ruined, and has irrationally hated the Colymar, blaming them for his misfortune.

- If an adventurer says that they examined the pasture before heading out, and makes a successful **Track** roll, they know that a half-dozen Greydogs took the cattle, judging from the tracks. A special success reveals that for some reason, they got into a scuffle near the bodies, then left. A critical success allows the tracker to later identify the murderer's boot-print.

When the players are ready to continue, the gamemaster can read or paraphrase the following:

The bandits were easy enough to follow—as it is impossible to disguise the path of three score cattle—but they took a strange detour northward, into these badlands where neither of your clans cares to venture. The grey and sullen sky overhead gives you no comfort in this bleak place, and any hope you had of returning home in fair weather is gone. Occasional drops of rain spatter upon you, and rumbling to the south indicates an oncoming storm.

Following the cattle-thieves' path, you have come across a disquieting sight…

The gamemaster should ask the adventurers each to attempt a **Scan** roll. Success means that the adventurers see a humanoid figure sprawled face-down on the ground several hundreds of meters to the north, lying amidst the vast swath of earth churned by cattle hoof-prints. A special or critical success reveals a small murder of crows pecking at the exposed flesh, indicating that the figure is quite dead. If no one succeeds in the **Scan** roll, they will stumble across the body as they follow the cattle's trail.

ONCE A KIN-SLAYER…

Approaching the body and looking closer reveals the body reveals that it is a human female, dark haired with brown eyes. A member of the Greydog clan, she is clad in the blue-edged woolen tunic characteristic to their weavers. Shooing the crows away, the adventurers can examine the body closer. Doing so, they learn that the woman's throat was cut, and she has nothing of value, the leather cords holding her coin-purse severed, and any weapons she carried have been taken. Only a small eating-knife is sheathed at her belt. Nearby her corpse is a ring of stones with the remnants of a fire.

A successful **Track** roll shows that she was killed, probably sitting at the fire, and was dragged away and abandoned. The tracks of the cattle cross over the path of the drag-marks, indicating that she was killed before the cattle were driven away. A special or critical success reveals that the boot-prints of her murderer were those of Danakos, the slayer of the Colymar herders.

A successful **Customs** roll reveals that this is highly uncharacteristic of the Greydog clan (as well as the Colymar), to kill one of their own and leave them face-down for crows to peck at, without digging a grave or even arranging the body respectfully. The adventurer succeeding in this roll may also recognize that the honorable thing to do would be to bury the Greydog's body. The ground is too rocky to dig a grave by hand—and the adventurers have few tools at their disposal—but gathering enough stones to cover her corpse is the work of only a quarter of an hour.

If she is with the adventurers, Yanioth could put her summoned earth elemental to use at this task.

THE TREES HAVE EYES

While (or if) the adventurers ponder the circumstances surrounding this murder, the gamemaster should ask for another **Scan** roll. Any that succeed notices movement off in the distance: someone is watching them, standing near a ragged copse of trees off to the west of the cattle-trail. If the adventurers shout out, beckon, or otherwise give any indication that they are aware of their observer, the figure darts away frantically, trying to make for the cover of some rock-filled gulleys on the other side of the copse of trees.

Giving pursuit should be no problem, as it becomes apparent that the figure is an old man in a loincloth and ragged cloak, frayed at the edges and patched crazy-quilt. A special success or critical success from the prior **Scan** roll reveals this at a distance, as well. The old man moves with the aid of a rough wooden staff, and his hair is matted and wild, and he keeps looking over his shoulders fearfully if the adventurers approach.

If the adventurers choose not to investigate or follow the man, the gamemaster should consult the section *On the Road to Ruins* on page 31. Left alone, the old man hides in a gully until the adventurers are long out of sight. Once the coast is clear, he emerges afterwards to approach the dead Greydog. Then, he attempts to put her spirit to rest, and return to his shack (described in *Shelter from the Storm*, page 30) where he continues his life as a hermit until his quiet and unceremonious death, years later.

Talking to the Old Man

If the old man is confronted or pursued, the adventurers get a better look at him (as described above). Knowing they're approaching, the he places his back against a rocky slope and gestures with his staff, warily trying to defend against any attackers.

- A successful **Intelligence Check** makes it clear that he is nearly blind, one eye milky white and the other squinting with effort. He's listening carefully to the movement of the adventurers on the rocky ground, as a means of tracking them.
- A successful **Area Lore (Dragon Pass)** roll lets an adventurer recognize him as a scavenger named Carthalo, known for scavenging items from the burial mounds and selling them in trading posts. He was long since driven away and has not been to the adventurer's village for years. A special success reveals that decades ago Carthalo was a reasonably proficient shaman and Daka Fal cultist from the Colymar area. He was driven mad in combat with a spirit, and has never been the same since.
- A successful **Luck Check** might even have an adventurer remember old Carthalo, having seen him several years ago.
- A successful use of **Fast Talk** can calm him down quickly, while **Orate** can be used if the adventurers have a lot of patience. Alternately, the gamemaster can simply allow the players to roleplay the encounter, and let the outcome determine how quickly Carthalo warms to the adventurers.

PLACES

The following locations are depicted on the map, but are outside the scope of this adventure.

- **Nymie Vale:** A settled area of small farms, vineyards, and pastures for cattle and sheep, claimed by the Colymar Tribe.
- **Clearwine Fort:** The main settlement of the Colymar tribe and the village of the Ernaldoring clan. The tribal king resides here. There is a weekly market, temples to the tribal gods, and many vineyards to the north and east.
- **Sacred Lands:** The vineyards and fields of the Earth Temple.
- **Earth Temple:** The main Earth Temple of this region: its high priestess is as important as any tribal king.
- **Arnoring Village:** Home of the Arnoring clan of the Colymar Tribe.
- **Quackford:** This market settlement is the main crossing of the Stream thanks to Sartar's Bridge, a

stone bridge built by Prince Sartar. Boats take goods from here all the way to Esrolia.
- **Old Tower:** An ancient fortification claimed by both the Colymar and the Lismelder tribes, currently empty.
- **Goodplate Inn:** Travelers between the Creek and the Stream can seek lodgings, food, and drink here.
- **Hillhaven:** Home of the Hillhaven clan of the Lismelder tribe.
- **Greydog Village:** Home of the Greydog clan of the Lismelder tribe, best known for the Greydog Inn, where travelers can seek lodging, food, and drink.
- **Little Starfire Ridges:** These steep cliffs are sacred to the Orlanth cult, and are claimed by the Orlmarth clan.
- **Badlands:** This region of the Starfire Hills is claimed by both the Colymar and Lismelder tribes. It is unsettled and considered good only for grazing sheep.
- **Broken Tower:** An old ruin in the Badlands of the Starfire Hills.

If one of the adventurers attacks him or tries to disarm him, he quickly drops his staff and calls to the spirits to welcome him. He is no combatant, and killing him brings no honor to the one who performs such an ill deed. Quite the opposite, as he may be able to summon some spirits to aid him or seek revenge for his death.

THE HERMIT OF THE BADLANDS

Once calmed and convinced the adventurers aren't the ones who came through earlier, or allied with them, he speaks freely. The gamemaster is encouraged to make Carthalo a bit of a challenge to talk with, as he's absent-minded and doesn't speak much to humans. Most of his conversation is with spirits, his god Daka Fal, the environment, and his own self, so he has lost some of the social skills such as recognizing conversational or behavioral cues. He's also hungry and has an eye for bright things, that would make nice offerings to the spirits inhabiting the badlands.

Carthalo knows who the Greydogs, the Lismelder, and the Colymar are, as he's lived his entire life in and between their territories. The gamemaster should make a **Reputation** for each adventurer from the area: if successful, Carthalo has heard of them. He may even remember the adventurer from their childhood.

It does not take much to win Carthalo over, and he shares what information he has.

- Carthalo fearfully mentions the "Stone Woman" as someone the adventurers should avoid, occasionally looks around frantically to see if she's within sight (she is not). *"Once in a while She stirs and walks the badlands, and that if you should see her, you should run."*
- He was foraging for roots when he saw the herd approach, and listened to them from afar as the Greydogs camped. The Stone Woman came to one of the Greydogs, and cast her spell upon him.
- That man went back into the camp and announced they were going north instead of back to Talavaldis, their home village. When they protested, he killed one of his own people. The rest then packed up and rode off, in the middle of the night. *"All of that happened since midnight, about half a day ago."*
- The Greydogs are probably taking the cattle to the Stone Woman's ruin, an ancient hilltop temple complex deep in the ragged forest and foothills to the north. The old ruin is not hard to find, and the wide swath of hoof-prints leads the adventurers right there.
- He doesn't know exactly what the Stone Woman is, but he avoids her, as she frightens him. He calls her that because she looks like the carved stone idols scattered here and there throughout the area.

Greydog Ghost

Examining the campsite with a successful **Track** roll reveals no sign of this Stone Woman. No recent human footprints other than those of the Greydogs and Carthalo are visible. No roll is required to tell where they went. The hoof-prints left a trail so obvious anyone could follow it.

As the adventurers talk with Carthalo, it becomes obvious that the weather is taking a turn for the worse. The clouds overhead darken, a light misty rain starts falling—not enough to drench anyone but enough to be uncomfortable.

CARTHALO

Daka Fal Shaman

Carthalo is a small wiry man, who often talks and mutters to people who aren't there. He is covered with countless tattoos and rarely wears more than a loincloth and an old patchwork wool cloak.

Carthalo obsessively fears that he is being watched and spied on by numerous things, including the idols of the Stone Woman, long-dead ghosts who feuded with his ancestors, by owls, and by a talking raccoon.

STR 11	CON 13	SIZ 11
INT 15	DEX 12	CHA 16
POW 18	Magic Points 18	

Location	D20	Armor/HP
Right Leg	01–04	0/5
Left Leg	05–09	0/5
Abdomen	09–11	0/5
Chest	12	0/6
Right Arm	13–15	0/4
Left Arm	16–18	0/4
Head	19–20	0/5

Weapon	%	Damage	SR	Pts
Quarterstaff	75	1D8	5	8

Runes: Moon 60%, Man 90%, Death 75%.
Rune Points: 6 (Daka Fal)
Passions: Loyalty (Ancestor Spirits) 80%.
Move: 8
Hit Points: 14
Armor: None.
Skills: Climb 60%, Jump 50%, First Aid 70%, Spirit Lore, Meditate 65%, Prepare Corpse 85%, Spirit Combat 95%, Search 60%, Listen 50%, Hide 50%, Move Quietly 50%.
Languages: Heortling 65%, Spiritspeech 70%, Tradetalk 25%.
Spirit Magic: Spirit Screen 6, Heal 5, Detect Enemies 1, Distraction 1, Befuddle 2.
Spirit Combat Damage: 1D6+3
Ransom: 500 L.
Shamanic Abilities: Carthalo can keep his Spirit Screen 6 spell effective indefinitely.
Taboo: Never wear any armor.
Magic Items: POW storage crystal holding 11 magic points.

Fetch: INT 13, POW 16, CHA 14
Skills: Spirit Combat 80%
Spirit Combat Damage: 1D6+2
Spirit Magic: Countermagic 4, Protection 3, Visibility 2, Dispel Magic 4

Carthalo says that the spirit of the dead Greydog woman should be put to rest, because he doesn't want another spirit wandering around lost in the badlands, especially if the Stone Woman might get to her. He tells the adventurers: *"The badlands are full of spirits and ghosts of all types. Most are just hungry for something, the same as anything else."*

Carthalo assures the adventurers that they'll be safe from the Stone Woman in his shack. The spirits of these badlands respect his desire to be left alone, and he has cleared the region of her menhir (standing stones) and idols.

If asked, he says that she is some sort of destructive goddess, associated with the Earth. Very old, born in the time of the Gods War. She is not a creature of Chaos, and in fact helped drive it out of the region. The Theyalans of old—original denizens of the area, whose language survives even still—used to worship her as some sort of earth deity, or—he thinks—as goddess of the herd.

Carthalo says that she's long asleep or dead, the only remnant is a ghost memory. There might be more than one of these Stone Women wandering the badlands... a goddess can have a lot of dreams over the centuries.

If the adventurers want to take part in this, they can participate with Carthalo. He asks any of them to assist with the preparation of the body for the ritual and for burial, requiring a successful **Prepare Corpse** roll. If the adventurers cannot do it, Carthalo walks them through it (or does it himself). Despite his apparently addled mind, he is still quite sharp when it comes to matters of death and the Spirit World.

In short order, the corpse is prepared, and Carthalo asks the adventurers to stand guard with him as he calls to the Greydog's ghost. To summon her ghost, Carthalo sits on the ground and begins a ritual chant, casting spells to summon her. Any of the adventurers able to help him are encouraged to do what they can, whether it be magical or even just chanting: even a successful roll of **Dance** or **Sing** can augment his chance of success.

If he is successful, the ghost of the Greydog shows up within an hour. With a special success, she arrives within ten minutes' time, and if the roll is a critical success, she shows up almost instantly and is immediately favorable to Carthalo and any assisting adventurers. If the summons is a failure, the Greydog's ghost does not appear. If it is a fumble, she appears in an enraged state, and is soon followed by a manifestation of the Stone Woman (see *The Dream of the Stone Woman* on page 33).

When the ghost of the Greydog appears, she is visible to everyone, appearing in her human guise. She has not yet gone into the Spirit World, and is stuck here in the badlands. Talking to spirits can be difficult, and this one is still in shock from the suddenness of her death and the strange and disquieting nature of these badlands, tainted as they are. Despite her rage at her former leader, she is still not overly fond of Colymar, and may require a **Customs**, **Fast Talk**, or **Oratory** to be coaxed into speaking to the adventurers.

Lannike Speaks

If she can be convinced to speak, she gives her name as Lannike Daughter of Leika of Snorri's Stead, and she tells the adventurers that she is remorseful for what happened. Though she has always followed Danakos' lead, she is not a murderer, and did not imagine that he would kill the herders. If it comes up that one of them survived, she immediately feels some measure of relief.

If Lannike is asked for an explanation of what happened, she says that with Danakos Son of Ergost, she and four other Greydogs—Mitrolar, Desonil, Theydinna, and Varanik—went along with his scheme, hoping to earn some fame and status within their clan with such a daring raid. They thought they'd simply ambush and tie up the Colymar herders, but Danakos surprised them by killing the captives. They argued, but it was too late. There was little they could do but return home with the cattle. She and the others made a pact that after they were rewarded by their clan chief, they'd return to the Colymar and offer to pay double the life price (ransom) for those that were killed.

Just before going to sleep, the other Greydogs confronted Danakos about their plan, and he said he'd watch the cattle and think about it. He woke them several hours later and said that they were to take the herd north, into the woods, a detour from the relatively easy path home. Lannike and the others refused, and the next thing she knew, she was coughing blood, and realized she'd been murdered.

The next few moments were a blur, and when she became aware of her surroundings once more, the cattle were gone. She tried to return to her village, but something about the nature of the badlands confused and disoriented her, and she has been looking for her kinsfolk ever since. Lannike begs Carthalo and any adventurers to put her spirit to rest.

The adventurers can either ignore her or they can agree to help her by resolving the issue that ties her to this world—revenge upon Danakos, rescue of her allies, and the restoration of the Colymar cattle. Once agreed, Carthalo shows her the way she must go once the matters that tie her to this world are resolved. She says she will wait by the gate, but points at a small rock on the ground, stained with her blood. Lannike tells them to throw it on the ground and she will come.

If they agree, Carthalo is favorably inclined to assist the adventurers. If they disagree and somehow do not allow Carthalo to set Lannike on the path to the higher worlds, she lets out a great wail of despair and attacks any who deny her this release. She has POW 12 and does 1D6 points of damage in **Spirit Combat** (see page 19). Carthalo is horrified by such callousness and refuses to deal with the adventurers any further, muttering that things have certainly changed with the Colymar.

The bloodstained rock, about the size of an egg, is otherwise unremarkable.

Shelter from the Storm

Once the spirit ritual is concluded, for better or for ill, Carthalo makes ready to depart, heading back to his home. Regardless of how he's been treated, he is not particularly interested in walking through the forest towards the Stone Woman's abode, so he'll part company with the adventurers. He might be convinced with a successful **Fast**

Talk or Orate roll, but likely changes his mind at the first sign of trouble. A special or critical success convinces Carthalo to stick with the adventurers to the bitter end, whatever that might be.

If the adventurers have sufficiently impressed him—or with a successful **Fast Talk** or **Orate** roll—Carthalo may offer the adventurers refuge in his domicile from the coming storm. He leads them to his place—a drafty but secure stone-walled shack tucked into the foothills, connected to a relatively shallow cave. On the way, the adventurers may notice a variety of warding runes and old glyphs inscribed and painted onto the ground, rocks, and into the trunks of the few trees in the area, living or dead. Also present are the signs of Daka Fal worship. Small totems have been arranged, and a successful **Intelligence Check** reveals that these are defensive wards against spirits.

Inside his hut is a bewildering clutter of pieces of pottery and cultural detritus, animal skulls and bones, colored stones carved with runes, bundles of dried and drying herbs, and the like. Items hang from the ceiling by twine or leather cords, but despite the chaos, the place is relatively clean. The shack is heated with a large fire-pit. Carthalo asks the adventurers to set the fire while he prepares some food. Once settled in, he'll feed them, give them some strips of dried lizard meat seasoned with salt and herbs, and bowls of thin and mostly unappetizing gruel made from local roots. He'll be overjoyed if the adventurers share their tastier provisions.

Riding the Storm Out

When the gathering storm intensifies and finally begins to unleash on the surrounding area, Carthalo asks them to tell of their past exploits. He does not get company and is unused to it, and asks a lot of questions.

When the time comes to sleep, Carthalo does not have anything more than his own bedroll, but offers it if asked. Everyone else can find a spot on the ground to sit—and to sleep—on as the storm rages outside. Any animals are penned in the front of the hovel, as is the custom. They spend a restless night, while rain pelts the surrounding countryside and lightning flashes, thunder cracking immediately overhead.

The next morning, Carthalo awakens them with the dawn. The storm has broken for the moment, but the sky is still bleak and spitting with a light rain, and there is a distant rumble throughout the hills and across the badlands, hinting at more of a storm to come.

If any of the adventurers have attempted to sway Carthalo, perhaps with successful use of the **Fast Talk** skill, the old hermit shaman might be convinced to go with them. However, he is terrified of the Stone Woman and if they encounter one of her stone markers and disrespectfully interfere with it, he abandons their company.

ON THE ROAD TO RUINS

Whether after finding the Greydog Lannike's corpse or after a night in Carthalo's shack, the adventurers eventually head northward in pursuit of the cattle, into the rocky foothills of the Starfire Mountain range. If they have chosen to go immediately,

they find that the storm intensifies as they go northward and the day darkens, and before long it is raining heavily. The stolen herd's tracks, nonetheless are easy to follow, and head several hours into the foothills, which grow increasingly thick with trees. If the adventurers wait for the next morning, they find that the trail has been washed away enough by the storm to require a successful **Track** roll at double the normal chance to find and follow it.

If they fail to find the tracks, they can continue to try, each attempting taking an hour. If they fail a second time, the gamemaster should state that they find the trail eventually, after a few hours of muddy searching.

As they move from the badlands into the rocky foothills, they see that the trail leads eventually to an ancient and long-abandoned road, the paving stones broken, separated over dozens of centuries of neglect, lost to mudslides and other calamities, but nonetheless a sign of onetime habitation. Noticeable are the many broken and defaced menhir (standing stones) along the road. All have been pushed over, broken apart, and the pieces scattered lazily.

None are intact enough to identify the subject, but a successful **Intelligence Check** by an adventurer paying attention reveals that they all depict the same subject, an extremely crude menhir carved to depict a thick-bodied woman, with her faceless head wreathed in bands, once standing as if watching over the road. The tallest were perhaps a meter and a half high, while the rest were roughly a meter tall. Closer examination of these, or a Detect Magic spell, determine that they are not magical, but probably were at some point in the past. Carvings on the obelisks (readable with a special success in **Read/Write Theyalan** or use of the Translate Rune spell) reveals that these are sacred stones, the goddess' "eyes", used to watch over the herds.

Should the adventurers wish to look for an intact menhir of the Stone Woman, they must make a wide search across the area as well as a successful **Search** roll. This slows them down considerably, versus the expedient course of following the trail left by the stolen herd. If they find one of these menhirs, it radiates magic for any with the ability to detect magic. If the adventurers attempt to damage or tamper with an intact menhir, the gamemaster should roll **POW×1** for each adventurer involved. Success means that a Stone Woman dream-weft materializes to investigate on SR 5, 30 meters away.

Consult *The Dream of the Stone Woman* sidebar (page 33) for more information.

A BELLOW FOR HELP

As the adventurers make their way through the rough woods under an increasingly turbulent cloud cover, the gamemaster should ask any who are riding point or taking care to scout the area to make either a **Listen** or a **Scan** roll (letting the players pick between them). Success yields a sign of one of their stolen cattle in the form of a frightened bellow and the clatter of hooves on stony ground (for **Listen**) or the sight of one of the steers rushing through the trees, pursued by a group of seven grey-skinned lizard creatures that race alongside it, leaping onto its back and biting at its flanks. It becomes visible to everyone when it is roughly 70 meters away.

A successful **Intelligence Check** roll identifies the creatures as rock lizards, trying to bring the

ROCK LIZARDS

These ponderous lizards are often found basking in the morning sun in the rocky plains of the badlands. Although carnivorous, they are too slow to catch most prey and feed mostly on carrion. They gather in groups up to a dozen. Rock lizard skin looks like grey rock and is quite tough, and when immobile, they can be mistaken for rocks.

STR 13	CON 13	SIZ 14
INT N/A	DEX 13	CHA N/A
POW 10	Magic Points 10	

Location	D20	Armor/HP
Tail	01–03	3/4
Right Hind Leg	04–05	3/6
Left Hind Leg	06–07	3/4
Hindquarters	08–11	3/6
Forequarters	12–15	3/6
Right Front Leg	16	3/4
Left Front Leg	17	3/4
Head	18–20	3/5

Weapon	%	Damage	SR
Claw (see below)	25	1D6+1D4	8
Bite (see below)	25	1D10+1D4	8

Combat: Rock lizards strike with both claws at once (roll twice) until one claw successfully hits, then they hold with that one, strike with the other, and bite on subsequent combat rounds.
Move: 4
Hit Points: 14
Base SR: 4
Armor: 3-point skin.
Skills: Smell Prey 50%, Hide 50%.

bull down and having only partial luck so far. Long runnels of blood paint the beeve's side, testament to their teeth and long claws. It is running out of energy and is lurching and stumbling as it charges, the fight almost gone out of it.

Should the adventurers hesitate too long, the rock lizards bring the bull down in two rounds, and do enough damage to kill it in the next two rounds. Should the adventurers interfere with the hunting pack, they have a fight on their hands, as the creatures are desperately hungry and fight until reduced to half hit points—at which point they'll run away—or until they are frightened away.

If this fight is going too easily for the adventurers, the gamemaster may wish to add additional rock lizards—more members of the pack, drawn by the cries—a few rounds later, up to a dozen or more.

If the Colymar bull is rescued, the adventurers may attempt to take care of it, using **Herd** to calm it, or even **First Aid** skill rolls and Heal spells to restore any lost hit points if it is sorely wounded. The adventurers can now continue upon their way, picking up the

trail where they left it, with one of their missing cattle in tow. On the bright side, only 59 cattle remain to be recovered.

As they continue, the destination of the Greydog clan becomes obvious, an old ruin standing on a steep hill, jutting upwards from the rocky hills and above the tree tops. A successful **Intelligence Check** reminds the adventurers that they cannot hear any birds any more, and the woods are strangely quiet, with the patter of light rain and wind blown leaves being the only sounds or movement. If they want to make **Scan** or **Listen** rolls, they can, but there is nothing to hear, nothing to see, other than the possible Stone Woman menhir, which are now more prevalent.

The trail of the herd and its thieves leads directly up a gently sloping ramp, into the old ruins.

THE OLD RUINS

At this point the adventurers may wish to do some reconnaissance or try to figure out what they can determine about the ruin. From a distance, they can see that it is a hilltop complex of some sort, walled and surrounded by smaller buildings. Most have crumbled, though a squat, cylindrical tower dominates, sticking up far above the walls, the only building in the whole complex more than a single story in height. Its roof is either collapsed or broken off, leaving it open to the sky.

- A successful **Scan** roll gives a quick sign of someone's head, peeking up over one of the walls. If the adventurers give any indication that they've seen the observer, it will drop back down and will not return. A special or critical success indicates it was a human male wearing an open-faced helm much like the one Lanneke wore, likely one of the Greydogs.
- A **Listen** roll catches the quick patter of footsteps echoing from the fort, likely from a human wearing boots. A special success lets an adventurer hear the lowing of cattle, while a critical success gives the adventurer the impression that the cattle are near the central building.
- If any of the adventurers have **Area Lore (Dragon Pass)**, a successful roll reveals that the old ruins and tower are supposedly a temple older than the Second Age, more than fifteen centuries old. The god or goddess worshipped here has long been forgotten, though.
- A successful **Battle** roll informs the adventurer that though the place would be a highly defensible position, the walls are not fortifications, and are not particularly well-suited for defense.
- **Herd** or **Animal Lore** reveal that the sloping path and ramp into the hilltop complex are well-designed for herding animals effectively. Rather than steps, it is a gentle ramp (though crumbling and weed-choked) and is dirt rather than stones.

Looking closer, the adventurers see that the wide, sloping ramp leads into the heart of the hilltop ruin. Should any choose to circle the hill, they see that a landslide wiped out a portion of the ruin, leaving the outer wall a jumbled pile of rubble scattered down the hillside, giving a clear and unblocked view of the squat tower in the center.

EXPLORING THE OLD RUINS

If the adventurers decide to search through the old ruins, there is a lot to see. Though the makers of the ruins have been gone for at least a thousand years, throughout its history various tribal groups and even bandit gangs have used it as a base, some appeasing Idrima and some being dragged to her altar and devoured. The ruins are half-exposed to the sky, and rubble chokes every narrow road and wrecked chamber, whole some few rooms or dwellings are intact.

Noticeably, the architecture is unlike anything the adventurers are familiar with, the shapes of the walls and organization of streets giving the disquieting sense of being built by something other than human. Dotting the area and spaced evenly along the ramp into the ruin are intact versions of the stone menhirs described on page 31, each depicting a heavy woman with exaggerated curves, bands of jewelry or something else encircling her head entirely. The stonework is relatively crude, well in keeping with the menhirs depicting the Stone Woman: hewn stones fitted tightly together, with little space between them, but no mortar. Other walls are much older, rough earthworks with exposed layers of gravel and stone.

Searching for the cattle requires a **Track** or **Listen** roll: success reveals that they are adjacent to the tower in the center of the temple complex, a short walk taking only around five minutes to find the way. If the roll is a failure, the adventurers become lost in the maze of ruins and must make a successful **Intelligence Check** to reorient themselves. A successful **Listen** roll near the broken tower reveals the sound of chanting (one voice, male) in the *Chamber of Offerings* (see page 34). Alternately, they can go straight to the cattle, penned in a large ceremonial corral (see page 38).

The skulls of cattle, bison, horse, rams, antelope, sable deer, and even impala litter the place, laying on the ground or even embedded curiously into earthy walls. A successful **Herd** roll reveals that some of these animals are not native to this region, while a successful **Animal Lore** roll identifies some of the more exotic species as musk oxen and aurochs.

Etched into the walls at various places in the old ruins are eye-high bands of inscriptions, pictures and runes made in Old Theyalan. These describe the birth of a demon-goddess—named Idrima—rising from the earth yet enfolded within it. The images, scattered throughout the ruined complex, describe Idrima's role as a protector of these lands against Chaos. The inscriptions show humans (from the Theyalan tribe, most likely) leading long lines of animals to Idrima's, depicted as described in *On the Road to Ruins*, page 31. This is likely the reason Carthalo thought she was a herd goddess. However, a successful **Intelligence Check** suggests that the herds are all led directly to her, versus her watching over them.

Maneuvering within the narrow, rubble-choked streets is not easy while mounted. Any **Ride** rolls made during combat situations are at a –20% while in the old ruin. A failed roll indicates the mount was blocked or unable to act as directed, and cannot attack or move in that turn. A fumble means the mount stumbles and the adventurer is thrown, requiring a successful **Agility Check** to avoid injury. Failing that causes the adventurer to take 1D6 points of damage.

Watchers in the Walls

Though they have no way of knowing it at the time, they are being watched the moment they enter the vicinity of the old ruins. Idrima uses her dream-wefts to manifest within her menhirs and observe anyone walking by, though she will use this ability sparingly as it is quite costly in terms of magic points. She can only manifest a few of them at any given time, though the ruins are small enough that they can manifest and roam freely within the hilltop confines.

More dangerous are the ancient guardians of the old ruin: her earth servitors, animated elemental beings called *sprul-pa* that can spawn "wearing" the animal skull they were created with. These creatures, long quiescent, are beginning to rise and become aware, watching from where they wait buried in the earth. If roused, they will manifest, seemingly climbing out of the ground under one of the animal skulls, which becomes their head. Interfering with any of the skulls has a 50% chance of summoning the nearest *sprul-pa*. If any of the adventurers interfere with the menhirs, she will call 1D4 *sprul-pa* to its defense, arriving on their SR the next round.

THE DREAM OF THE STONE WOMAN

If the adventurers are unlucky enough to attract the attention of the Stone Woman, either through the ritual to put the Greydog to rest or through interfering with one of her intact menhirs, Idrima stirs to partial awareness from her resting place in the broken tower, and spins a dream-weft to send forth and manifest in the real world.

The dream-wefts appear in her form as the Stone Woman, identical to the statues: a heavy woman clad in a billowing, hooded cloak of tattered grey finery, her face wrapped in loose bands (like bandages) with a single gleaming light emanating from between the bands. Her hands are clasped before her, long loose sleeves concealing even a trace of skin from sight. The cloak moves unnaturally, concealing her disturbing form.

She has a low, sultry voice, and has the same skills and languages as in her physical form. Rather than attempting to dominate and destroy those she faces in spirit combat, the Stone Woman simply wishes them to worship—and ultimately, feed—her, coaxing them to her tower.

See the writeup of Idrima on page 39 for her attributes and languages. However, her dream-wefts are simpler creatures, little more than ethereal entities with the semblance of form, capable of communication, Spirit Combat, and the use of her Enthrall ability. The dream-wefts have INT and DEX equal to Idrima's, while their POW is merely 1D6+6, with magic points equal to POW.

Dream-wefts will enter spirit combat if threatened. See page 39 for more information. They can be destroyed easily, and are more likely to flee back to the statue they emanated from, rather than sticking around for a prolonged encounter. Idrima uses her dream-wefts as messengers, spies, and lures, rather than as combatants.

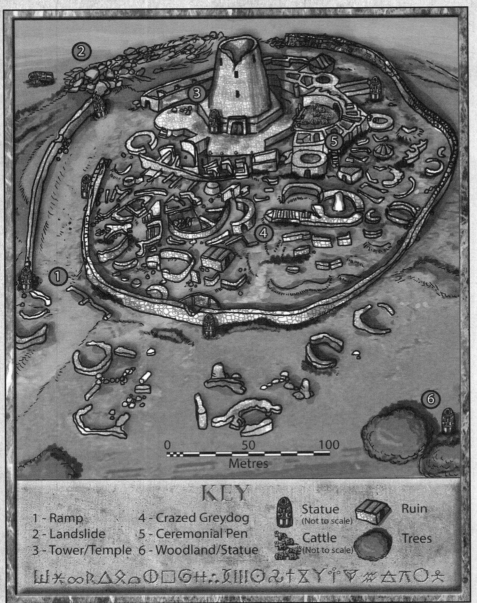

KEY

1 - Ramp 4 - Crazed Greydog
2 - Landslide 5 - Ceremonial Pen
3 - Tower/Temple 6 - Woodland/Statue

Statue (Not to scale) Ruin

Cattle (Not to scale) Trees

0   50   100

Metres

buildings, terrified of everything. Every five minutes the characters are in the ruins, the gamemaster should roll against the **POW×1** of the adventure with the lowest POW. If this roll is a success, Varanik tries to target that adventurer, either directly attacking them from an attempted ambush, throwing a rock or spear at them, or pushing over some piece of stone wall onto the adventurer. Varanik is described on page 35.

Exploring the Ruins

If the adventurers announce that they are trying to find anything of value, the gamemaster should allow each adventurer to attempt one **Search** roll every 5 minutes. Failing this roll means that the adventurer finds nothing; a success merits a d20 roll on the **Loot** table (see page 41). A special success allows a roll of 1d10 on the table, and the gamemaster should roll 1d6 if the roll is a critical success. Once an item is discovered, the gamemaster should instead use result 20.

The Chamber of Offerings

The central chamber of the broken tower is a round room with sloping walls, deep alcoves set into them. Only one door leads to and from the room: the one the adventurers are at. The tower's roof collapsed long ago, and piles of rubble were pushed to the sides of the central chamber, or have been shoved outside by the door. Whatever light there is (depending on the time of day) shines directly down on the low stone altar in the center of the room, illuminating a flensed and bloody horned bull skull sitting in its midst, with an array of reddened bones arranged in a strange pattern beneath it and a bloody cow-hide draped over one side. Rain drips down, making all shine with wetness.

Behind the altar is three-meter high ochre-stained stone statue of a giant naked woman, her female characteristics exaggerated to a grotesque degree. The altar is already stained with blood and gore, the copper scent of blood permeating everywhere. A closer look at the altar reveals that it is essentially an open ended cylinder, filled to the brim with earth. On the ground next to this altar are ragged chunks of one of the stolen Colymar bulls, crudely butchered.

Nearby, sprawled and slumped against one wall are the three Greydogs as-of-yet unaccounted for—Mitrolar, Desonil, and Theydinna (if the adventurers have not yet met Varanik they will notice that a fourth Greydog is missing). The Greydogs' throats were cut, their chests drenched with blood, and their garments showing signs of a struggle. It is obvious that they were sacrificed

Those within earshot come without any magic points, while she can call more at a cost of 1 magic point per servitor.

The *sprul-pa* move through the earth, leaving a slight ripple in their wake as if moving just under the surface of water, and can also move through earthen walls, of which there are plenty. See *Servants of the Earth Goddess* (following) for more information about the *sprul-pra*. So far, only a few of the Colymar cattle have been turned into sprul-pa. The gamemaster might indicate that though most are filthy dirt-caked hides and old yellowing bone, these few have "fresh" bloody skulls and hides, perhaps even horns marked with signs that will be obvious to the adventurers.

The other potential encounter within the ruin is Varanik, one of Danakos' followers, the last of the Greydogs mentioned by Lannike. Idrima attempted to enthrall him and drove her crazy, and he is trying to avoid her notice, darting to and fro throughout the buildings, hoping one of his allies will find him and take him to safety. Varanik took part in Danakos' sacrifice of his friends, and the experience broke him. He's now covered in dried blood, darting in and out of the ruined

SPRUL-PA

Servants of the Earth Goddess

Over the centuries, Idrima has made dozens of mindless servitors, conjured out of earth combined with the bones, hide, and heads of animals sacrificed to her. A *sprul-pa* appears as a roughly human-sized thing, covered in bloody vines, and with the head of a dead cow or bull, held together with vines and sticks. The *sprul-pa* are not undead, and are more akin to Earth elementals. The name *sprul-pa* is an ancient one, meaning "conjured thing," and is not specific to these creatures.

These servitors lack CON and thus total hit points. If a limb is broken or smashed, the servitor continues fighting as best it can. If its head is destroyed, the *sprul-pa* ceases to act.

STR 15	CON N/A	SIZ 11
INT N/A	DEX 11	CHA N/A
POW 7	Magic Points 7	

Location	D20	Armor/HP
Right Leg	01–04	1/1
Left Leg	05–09	1/1
Abdomen	09–11	1/1
Chest	12	1/1
Lower Right Arm	13	1/1
Lower Left Arm	14	1/1
Upper Right Arm	15–16	1/1
Upper Left Arm	17–18	1/1
Head	19–20	4/4

Weapon	%	Damage	SR	Pts
Right Claw	55	1D6+1+1D4	9	—
Left Claw	55	1D6+1+1D4	9	—

Combat Notes: A *sprul-pa* can claw the same opponent twice in the same melee round. The *sprul-pa* initially uses its upper arms to attack. If an upper arm is destroyed, it continues to attack with the lower arm.
Move: 8
Base SR: 5
Armor: 1-point hide over limbs and body, 4-point bone and horns on head.
Skills: Dodge 33% (equal to DEX×3)
Earth Passage: On SR 5, a *sprul-pa* can spend 1 magic point and descend into the ground, sinking to the level of its skull, which becomes detached if the *sprul-pa* moves away or goes deeper than surface level. It can move its normal MOV while buried. It can also do this with soil walls, at which point the skull drops to the ground. Like a hermit crab switching shells, it can only re-emerge from the earth into a skull—its own or another on SR 5 of the next available round. It must spend 1 magic point per round to move, but does not need to spend any magic points to remain immobile. Most of the skulls in the old ruin were *sprul-pa* at one point or another, and at any given time, there will be 1D6–1 usable skulls within 10 meters of any given adventurer.

VARANIK

Greydog Cattle Thief

Varanik is the sole survivor of the cattle-raiding group, save for Danakos, who has become Idrima's slave. His mind snapped due to a fumble when he tried to resist her Enthrall ability, and now he scurries around the ruins, wild-eyed and muttering to himself, terrified of the Stone Woman. He may have helped Danakos kill his fellow Greydogs: the blood on his weapons and armor certainly suggests that he has been up to something. His lowered INT and CHA are due to his confused, paranoid state.

Varanik does not need to fight to the death, and in fact would rather prefer to live. He might give up if seriously injured. An **Insight (Human)** roll reveals that he's wracked with guilt and temporarily maddened, and a **Fast Talk** roll could potentially talk him down long enough for some sort of healing to be attempted.

STR 14	CON 14	SIZ 14
INT 13 (6)	DEX 11	CHA 12 (6)
POW 12	Magic Points 12	

Location	D20	Armor/HP
Right Leg	01–04	3/5
Left Leg	05–09	3/5
Abdomen	09–11	3/5
Chest	12	3/6
Right Arm	13–15	3/4
Left Arm	16–18	3/4
Head	19–20	4/5

Weapon	%	Damage	SR	Pts
Battleaxe	60	1D8+2+1D4	8	8
Medium Shield	55	1D4+1D4	8	12
Javelin	50	1D8+1D2	3	8

Runes: Air 75%, Movement 70%.
Rune Points: 3 (Orlanth Adventurous)
Passions: Loyalty (Greydog Clan) 60%.
Move: 8
Hit Points: 15
Armor: Quilted linen hauberk (3 pts.), cuirboilli greaves and vambraces (3 pts.), open helm (4 pts.).
Skills: Ride 25%, Climb 50%, Jump 50%, Battle 30%, First Aid 40%, Herding 65%, Farm 60%, Spirit Combat 50%, Scan 40%, Listen 50%, Hide 45%.
Languages: Heortling 65%, Tradetalk 25%.
Spirit Magic: Bladesharp 2, Strength 2, Heal 3, Protection 2.
Treasure: Back in Talavaldis, he has 1 hide of land, and wants more.
Ransom: 500 L.

If any of the adventurers took the bloodstained stone from the ground where Lannike was slain and remember it at this point, they might remember to throw it to the ground, at which point Lannike's ghost will materialize on the spot. Her sudden spectral appearance could be utilized to calm Varanik for a moment, appealing to his loyalty to the Greydog clan, or her manifestation can potentially be used as a distraction, confronting Danakos and even spurring him to regret or as a feint to gain an opportunity for a killing blow.

The gamemaster is encouraged to improvise these potential interactions, providing suitable emotional weight for the confrontation.

here, and any familiarity with sacrifice means that their magic points have likely gone somewhere.

A strangely curving array of rivulets leading from the altar are full of blood, draining into holes set in the floor at various places in the room. Arrayed throughout the room at the edges of the floor are stone bowls of all shapes and sizes, high and low. Some of them have shriveled and unidentifiable bits of material in them, others are empty, while others are full of bloody flesh and cow-hide, cut from the skull on the altar. Skulls of animals litter the floor, as well, each a potential spawning point for one of Idrima's *sprul-pa*.

Behind the altar and the dead bull looms the statue, the true form of the Stone Woman, though without her enfolding cloak and robe. The statue's arms are folded at its sides and the oversize head is featureless but for the knobbed bands that run entirely around it. The legs end in toes that splay like roots, and the stony surface is entirely stained in ochre.

The adventurers are no strangers to animal sacrifice, as it is commonly practiced, but the sort of ritual offerings they have always witnessed and taken part in are generally more ceremonial in nature. There is the sense that this was something more primitive, more primal, and the chamber itself is disquieting beyond their experience.

The Traitor at Last

The gamemaster should make a roll for Danakos' **Hide** skill. He has concealed himself behind a pile of rubble, having heard their approach and battles with the cattle-skulled *sprul-pa*. The gamemaster should ask each of the adventurers to attempt a **Listen** or **Scan** roll (player choice), opposed by the results of Danakos' Hide roll. If his Hide is successful and the adventurers do not notice him, he attempts an ambush, using **Move Quietly** to try to get the first strike in to whomever he judges the most dangerous. If they attempt any sign of interfering with his work on the altar—readying the construction of a new *sprul-pa* for Idrima—he leaps to the attack, and should present a startling figure, spattered in dried blood, dirt, and gore.

Danakos is not interested in any parlay with the adventurers. He knows that should they return with him as a captive, his life is forfeit. He has murdered Colymar and Greydogs in cold blood, acts beyond any redemption or life-payment. At best, his destiny is exile from his homeland, but most likely his fate is to be executed for his crimes. As he fights, he urges Idrima to anger, promising her the Colymar cattle, the adventurers themselves, and more besides.

Danakos urges his goddess to manifest.

THE STONE ALSO RISES

The presence of outsiders in the chamber has the unfortunate circumstance of awakening Idrima, who immediately begins by spending 6 magic points to awaken the fresh *sprul-pa* prepared by Danakos. It will appear on strike rank 11. The servitor seemingly climbs up from within the earth into the arrangement of bones, hide, and skull, with vines growing rapidly to encompass it. It is not immediately hostile, however, and watches them, observing the adventurers while other *sprul-pa* begin to awaken and appear in the immediate vicinity, outside the Chamber of Offerings.

The Stone Woman begins to stir, revealing to the adventurers that the great, grotesque altar is not a depiction of the goddess, but Idrima herself. She speaks first in Earthtongue, announcing in a low voice that sounds as if it comes from many mouths at once: *"I awaken. I hunger. I have slept for far too long! I thirst for blood and offerings! Will you bring me more?"*

If they do not understand or reply to her, she will repeat the same message in Old Theyalan, then Heortling. She does not move to attack, and instead behaves as if she expects to be given offerings and shown due respect. The adventurers can avoid a bloody conflict if they choose to parley with her. As a chthonic entity, Idrima is not overly interested in combat, and does not need anything the adventurers have on their persons. Danakos has served her well for the last day or so, but loyal servants are not overly rare when one can Enthrall.

If Carthalo is present, he recognizes her power for what it is and urges caution. He'll admit to fear about having Idrima awake and active, but if she is willing to keep Chaos at bay, he can accommodate her presence into his world. If she asks, he even promises to make sacrifices to her now and again, to keep her pacified.

Dealing with the Demon-Goddess

How the adventurers deal with Idrima and the situation is entirely up to them, as her goal is solely to be fed, and she is not particularly aggressive or malicious. She is not a creature of Chaos, and despite being a "demon" she is not interested in the pursuit of evil, merely selfishness when it comes to her survival.

- **Fighting:** If they adventurers are bold, they can fight Idrima, leading to a climactic battle as she manifests and throws her considerable power at them, summing *sprul-pa* and evoking dream-wefts. The demon-goddess is tough, but not undefeatable. As described above, she can merge into the Earth and has dozens of *sprul-pa* at her disposal. The dream-wefts are relatively weak, but can provide distractions. Her combination of physical strength, earthquake abilities, and fearsome gaze make her formidable, but clever tactics, luck, and resourcefulness can turn the tide against her.
- **Fleeing with the Cattle:** The adventurers can attempt to just cut and run, killing Danakos Son of Ergost, killing their way past Idrima's guardians, and trying to get the remaining cattle out before her creatures can tear them all apart. This resolution is bound to be bloody and chaotic, with Idrima boiling out of the broken tower in a last-ditch effort to stop them.
- **Fleeing without the Cattle:** If the adventurers choose to just flee without attempting to rescue the cattle, they are certainly

DANAKOS, SON OF EGROST

Greydog Cattle Thief

Danakos Son of Egrost is an ambitious warrior of the Greydog clan, who has earned a name for himself raiding other clans. A skilled warrior, Danakos is also a self-interested bully. He has been possessed by Idrima and is under her psychic control, his loyalty to her due to her Enthrall ability. Danakos' sanity has been shattered by the crimes he has committed under Idrima's influence.

In combat, Danakos first tries to Demoralize a foe and then casts protective magic upon himself before casting Fanaticism. He fights recklessly, without any hope for survival, casting as many offensive spells as he can muster, eschewing any defensive actions other than those that let him fight further. He neither gives quarter nor asks for it. He will not cast any Rune magic, due to Idrina's influence.

STR 15	CON 14	SIZ 15
INT 13	DEX 12	CHA 14
POW 14	Magic Points 14	

Location	D20	Armor/HP
Right Leg	01–04	3/5
Left Leg	05–09	3/5
Abdomen	09–11	3/5
Chest	12	3/6
Right Arm	13–15	3/4
Left Arm	16–18	3/4
Head	19–20	4/5
Upper Left Arm	17–18	1/1
Head	19–20	4/4

Weapon	%	Damage	SR	Pts
Broadsword	75	1D8+1+1D4	8	12
Medium Shield	60	–	–	12
Javelin	60	1D8+1D2	3	–

Runes: Air 85%, Movement 75%, Disorder 85%.
Rune Points: 4 (Orlanth Adventurous)
Passions: Loyalty (Idrima) 90%, Loyalty (Greydog Clan) 60%, Honor 60%, Hate (Colymar Tribe) 60%.
Move: 8
Hit Points: 15
Armor: Quilted linen hauberk (3 pts.), cuirboilli greaves and vambraces (3 pts.), open helm (4 pts.).
Skills: Ride 45%, Climb 60%, Jump 60%, Battle 40%, First Aid 50%, Herd 60%, Scan 60%, Listen 50%, Hide 50%, Move Quietly 50%.
Languages: Heortling 65%, Tradetalk 25%.
Spirit Magic: Bladesharp 3, Demoralize 2, Heal 3, Fanaticism 1, Protection 2.
Ransom: Unknown (normally 500 L).

able to do so. Idrima and her creatures will menace them out of the hilltop ruins, but will not attempt to detain them overmuch. Once they're gone, Danakos will sacrifice more of the cattle to make fresh *sprul-pa* for her, and eventually she will let him go, allowing him to return to his home village with a third of the herd to show for his efforts. The adventurers, meanwhile, will meet a cool reception back at home, and may find that they've lost a lot of favor.

- **Bargaining:** Lastly, and perhaps most sensibly, the adventurers can bargain with the demon-goddess, negotiating to give her some share of the cattle (she will demand half, but will settle for a third). Perhaps she could be convinced to take someone else's cattle in return, which might set off another cycle of cattle-theft and reprisal. She is not overly interested in human sacrifice, other than as a source for magic points. Maybe she wants more than that, perhaps something needs to be restored? Ultimately, the adventurers may realize that she is not particularly evil… she's just hungry and used to getting her way. Perhaps the adventurers need to swear an oath to make sure each tribe stays off Idrima's territory, or must negotiate through Varanik or Danikos, if either is alive and freed from madness and possession. Yanioth, the priestess of Ernalda might even object to killing Idrima, as her chthonic earth-goddess nature makes her a potential ally to Ernalda. Idrima has no particular affection for her wefts or servitors, and does not begrudge their destruction.

There is no single solution to this adventure, no "correct" means of dealing with Idrima. The adventurers can destroy her, earning glory and increasing their Reputation in the process, or they can appease her somehow by offering to live and let live. They can make an alliance with her, giving the Colymar a significantly powerful ally in the Hero Wars to come, and a distinct advantage over the hated Lismelder clan. Each has its benefits and drawbacks, but regardless of which path is followed, the adventurers will have taken part in an epic new change in the power dynamics of the area, and added an interesting note to their own journeys towards hero-dom.

THE CEREMONIAL CORRAL

With Idrima and Danakos dealt with, the adventurers will almost certainly wish to find the missing Colymar cattle. They are penned into a large corral, choked with weeds, and blocked with a stone gate that has survived the millennia intact, balanced on a pivot and sliding back and forth into place. Exactly 54 of the creatures remain in this corral, with one lost and encountered by the adventurers earlier, and five sacrificed to Idrima and turned into *sprul-pa* (see page 35).

A successful **Herd** roll will be required to get them gathered and moving out of the pen, through the temple complex and down the hill, made difficult if the adventurers are hindered by attacks from the *sprul-pa* or the demon-goddess herself.

REWARDS AND EXPERIENCE

Restoring the cattle to the Colymar clan earns a bonus of +3% Reputation, modified by any of the following:

- +1% Reputation for killing Idrima.
- +2% Reputation for negotiating a pact of alliance with her.
- +1% Reputation for capturing Danakos and/or Varanik and ransoming them back to the Greydogs.

In addition to the social rewards, the adventurers will also be able to keep any treasures they found in the old ruin, and can keep any money they make from ransoming Danakos and/or Varanik. Zarah, the Colymar clan chieftain's wife, rewards them each with 200 L as thanks, or the equivalent in cattle or other benefits the clan can provide.

Idrima the Stone Woman summoning her Earthquake Stomp.

IDRIMA, THE STONE WOMAN

Demonic Earth Goddess

Idrima is one of the many daughters of Maran Gor the Earthshaker, born to that goddess when blood was first spilled upon the Earth in the Gods War. Idrima fought the enemies of Earth such as Chaos and trolls, and others who angered the Earth goddesses. Idrima can be appeased and calmed with blood—either that of her victims or that offered to her in sacrifice. During the Great Darkness, she helped to keep Chaos away from this area. At the Dawn, the local Theyalans worshiped Idrima as a guardian and protector and offered her sacrifices of animals and humans, but her cult died out as the blessings of the Dawn grew. Neglected, she went to sleep deep in the Earth. She has reawakened, thirsty for blood. Idrima is a cult spirit of the Earth goddesses (and thus could be subject to Yanioth's Command Cult Spirit spell), and could even be potentially worshiped as a subcult of Maran Gor.

Idrima appears as a huge female seemingly carved from stone and covered with red ochre. She is obviously female, with exaggerated thighs, hips, belly, and breasts. Her arms are thick, jointed tentacles with smaller branches beneath, serving as fingers, her feet similar, almost resembling roots. Her head is disproportionately small and faceless; instead it is covered in horizontal circular bands, but when she is roused, the bands open and reveal a great staring eye the size of her entire head. When motionless, she can easily be mistaken for a statue.

Her magic points are higher due to the recent sacrifice of the three Greydogs, and she has spent some of these making new sprul-pa.

STR 25	CON 13	SIZ 25
INT 13	DEX 13	CHA 19
POW 25	Magic Points: 36 (normally 25)	

Location	D20	Armor/HP
Right Leg	01–03	6/8
Left Leg	04–06	6/8
Abdomen	07–10	6/9
Chest	11–15	6/10
Right Arm	16–17	6/7
Left Arm	18–19	6/7
Head	20	6/7

Weapon	%	Damage	SR	Pts
Grab	80%	2D3 + (see below)	7	12
Crushing Embrace	Auto	2D6/round	1	12
Earthquake Stomp	Auto	See below	3	–
Faceless Gaze	Auto	See below	3	
Enthrall	POW vs. POW	See below	3	

Move: 7
Hit Points: 23
Base SR: 3
Armor: 6-point stone skin.
Runes: Earth 100%, Disorder 90%.
Skills: Spirit Combat 90%, Speak Old Theyalan 90%, Speak Heortling 45%, Speak Earthtongue 100%, Speak Spiritspeech 50%.
Spirit Combat Damage: 2D6+3

Combat: Each round Idrima tries either to *Grab* an adventurer or use her *Earthquake Stomp* or *Faceless Gaze* attacks. If she successfully *Grabs* an adventurer, she may make a *Crushing Embrace* attack on that adventurer each successive round. If no adventurer is grabbed or within range, she will use her *Earthquake Stomp* or *Faceless Gaze*.

Grab: Once per round, Idrima can try to grab an adventurer. Once Grabbed, an adventurer must overcome Idrima's STR to be freed (or somehow incapacitate her right Arm). Idrima can only grab one adventurer at a time. The following round a Grabbed adventurer receives the *Crushing Embrace*.

Crushing Embrace: The *Crushing Embrace* begins the round after an adventurer has been Grabbed by Idrima. Each round, the adventurer receives 2D6 damage to the chest. Armor protects until it is overcome. Idrima keeps crushing an adventurer until either the adventurer overcomes Idrima's STR, incapacitates Idrima's arm, convinces Idrima to release the adventurer, or the adventurer is reduced to 2 or fewer hit points.

Earthquake Stomp: Any round that Idrima does not make a *Grab* or *Faceless Gaze* attack, she can stomp the ground with her foot, causing a small earthquake. The *Earthquake Stomp* affects 9 square meters around Idrima. Everyone within that area must subtract –15% from all Agility and Manipulation skills and DEX rolls for the next full round. Each round, anyone standing up must succeed in a DEX×5 roll (at a –15% penalty) or fall prone.

Faceless Gaze: Any round Idrima does not make a *Grab* or *Earthquake Stomp* attack, she can turn her Faceless Gaze upon an adventurer, opening the bands of flesh that wreath her great staring-eye. If she overcomes her target's POW with her own, the victim acts in all ways as if Demoralized for the next 10 minutes. If Idrima gets a special success, the victim collapses for a number of full turns equal to 20 minus the victim's CON. If she gets a critical success, the victim not only collapses as above, but must make a CON×5 roll or die immediately from sheer shock and terror. Her *Faceless Gaze* is the equivalent of a 1-point Rune spell for purposes of defensive magic.

Dream-wefts: She may spend 1 magic point to create a dream-weft. Each takes a full combat round to create, and they seem to emanate from the altar as grayish, ochre-streaked mist, then coalesce into something resembling Idrima's cloaked Stone Woman form. The dream-weft then descends into the earth and re-emerges at one of her menhirs. See page 33 for more information on the dream-wefts.

Sprul-pa: Idrima can summon a sprul-pa to her at the cost of 1 magic point and 5 strike ranks, from anywhere within the old ruin, with the servitor manifesting at one of the skulls. If the creature is already present and manifest (50% chance of one being within earshot), she can simply call to it in

Earthtongue, without needing to spend any magic points. This takes 5 strike ranks, and 1D4 *sprul-pa* arrive the next round on their strike rank.

Enthrall: When not in combat, Idrima may spend 6 magic points to enthrall a potential target, causing them to serve and protect her. This is resolved as a resistance roll of Idrima's POW versus the intended target's POW, though she cannot do this against targets that are actively hostile towards her. If successful, the subject is enthralled, temporarily assigned a temporary passion of Loyalty (Idrina) 90%, serving her for one full day. On a special success, the time extends to 1D3+3 days, and a critical success gives her one full season of service. An enthralled victim asked to do something they would normally be opposed to (such as fighting friends, betraying oaths, etc.) can attempt a roll of POW×3 to break free of the enthrallment. This roll should be augmented with relevant passions (gamemaster's discretion). If the enthrallment is broken, the Loyalty (Idrina) is removed. The spirit magic spells Countermagic and Dispel Magic

Menhir depicting Idrima the Stone Woman.

will work against *Enthrall*, as will the rune spells Absorption, Dismiss Magic, or Inviolable can also negate the effects of Enthrall.

Magic: At SR 3 of any round, Idrima can merge into the earth and stone surrounding her, whether wall or ground. When so merged, she cannot be attacked physically, nor can she attack except through Spirit Combat or *Faceless Gaze*. This process causes her to slough off much of her body, leaving an ochre stain and an unpleasant gritty slime in her wake. It takes her a full day and a night to reform her body (even if it has been destroyed).

Idrima can Discorporate at SR 3 of any round she has not already acted in, and send her spirit around to attack through Spirit Combat or *Faceless Gaze*. While Discorporate, her body is vulnerable unless she has merged with her surroundings.

Furthermore, as a chthonic earth-goddess, Idrima is able to absorb magic points from sacrifices made to her, and will not be attacked by creatures of the earth, such as an earth elemental. If she encounters one, she can speak to it in Earthtongue and enter a POW vs. POW resistance roll to take control of it, guiding it as if it were under her command.

RUNEQUEST VETERAN?

If the players are familiar with prior editions of RUNEQUEST, this adventure can be used without much difficulty for adventurers created using prior editions. The rules portion of this adventure contains enough information to explain passions, Runes, and other changes to the system, and the RUNEQUEST system is flexible enough that characters can be quickly adapted to use these rules, or they can be ignored. A group familiar with HEROQUEST should have even less trouble adapting this adventure to that rules set.

All that's important is that this adventure is suitable for a relatively inexperienced group of initiate-level adventurers—Rune Lords or Rune Priests are probably too powerful—and that the adventurers have some reason for being in the Dragon Pass area.

Alternately, the events and locale of this adventure are isolated enough that it can be placed almost anywhere in Genertela, or elsewhere on Glorantha as desired.

Roll	Result
1	A small golden figure of an unknown god. A successful **Appraise** roll reveals that it is worth at least 150 L. No Lore skills, even if successful, can identify the god. Sometimes it is important to accept the unknown.
2	A small metal and crystal phial, still closed, filled with gray powder. This powder can remove any current disease, magic or otherwise, if mixed with wine and imbibed, requiring half a day to take effect. There are 1Dd6 doses of the powder, and a successful **Medicine** or **Alchemy** roll will identify these properties, but such analysis will consume one of the doses.
3	A fist-sized idol of the Stone Woman fashioned out of dull grey stone (see page 39 for a description of Idrima). It doubles as a magic point storage crystal, with a capacity of 8 magic points. It is currently empty.
4	A small knife carved from mottled red and green stone, polished brightly, its edge still razor-keen. **Mineral Lore** identifies it as jasper. Once the hilt was wrapped with something, likely leather cord, but it is desiccated and flakes away when touched. It is worth perhaps 50 L.
5	A bronze cloak-pin with a large square plate of blue jade, its provenance unknown. Wearing this exotic keepsake can increase an adventurer's Reputation by +1%.
6	Several shards of opalescent milk quartz, carved with strange glyphs. These can be fitted together and deciphered with a successful roll of **Read/Write Old Theyalan**. Deciphering these glyphs for a full day gives the adventurer a one-time bonus of +1D3% to Old Theyalan.
7–8	A jawbone filled with teeth that have been replaced entirely with silver pins driven into the bone and set with semi-precious minerals. No apparent use other than as a conversation piece. Value 250 L.
9–10	A rotten leather bag containing almost a dozen small pieces of colored minerals, each about the size of a finger-tip, carved figures of men, women, children, and dragonnewts, with some smaller rounded tokens. A successful **Empire of Wyrm's Friends Lore** roll identifies this as a popular children's boardgame. The board was a piece of cloth, now rotted away. A critical success lets the adventurer remember the rules. The set is worth about 200 L to a collector, maybe 50 L for the value of the stones.
11–13	A ring carved out of black marble. Worth 75 L.
14–16	Once this was a hide and wood quiver, but now it is a long mushy stain with a bunch of arrowheads clustered at one end. The arrowheads are chipped out of obsidian and aren't worth much, but are still functional.
17–19	A fairly recent small clay pot stoppered with red wax, the inside filled with slick grey material. This was once a healing unguent, but has now gone bad. If smeared on a wound, it will delay the healing process by 1 week, itching fiercely, and cause magical healing to have 1 less point of effectiveness, per wound.
20	Broken shards of pottery with glazes of unusual hues, or a crushed blob of verdigrised bronze, with no obvious purpose. Valueless to any except an archaeologist.

VASANA, DAUGHTER OF FARNAN

Veteran heavy cavalrywoman of the Ernaldori clan of the Colymar Tribe.
Female, age 21. Initiate of Orlanth Adventurous.

Introduction: *I am Vasana, the daughter of Farnan, a hero of Starbrow's Rebellion, slain and devoured by the Crimson Bat. In my war of revenge against the Lunar Empire, I gained the attention of Argrath at the Battle of Pennel Ford. I was sorely wounded at the Second Battle of Moonbroth, granting me this terrible scar across on the left half of my face. I returned to my mother's farm to recover, and now I am ready for adventure. My friends know me for a fearsome bison rider, a skilled hand with a sword, and a devout worshipper of Orlanth Adventurous. My honor is my greatest strength.*

Vasana is a small but athletic woman with red-hair and a vicious scar across her left face. Despite her small size, she rides a bison and is more than capable of commanding warriors and priests more senior than herself.

Vasana's grandmother was a scribe in the service of the Princes of Sartar, and died with great glory in the Battle of Boldhome. Vasana's father was Farnan, a temple orphan who married Vareena, a priestess of Ernalda from the Ernaldori clan. Farnan joined Starbrow's Rebellion and later personally aided Kallyr Starbrow in her escape from Sartar. He died defending Whitewall in 1620, devoured by the Crimson Bat. Farnan's soul was annihilated and Vasana, then a teenager, swore revenge.

As soon as she was initiated as an adult, Vasana left her mother's farm to avenge her father against the Lunar Empire. In 1623, she followed King Broyan to the metropolis of Nochet, accompanied by her half-sister Yanioth. At the Battle of Pennel Ford, she fought with great glory, and gained the attention of Argrath. Vasana followed Argrath into Prax and joined the army of the White Bull in the liberation of Pavis. Pursuing honor again, she fought with great glory at the Second Battle of Moonbroth, and was nearly killed (receiving a nasty scar across her left eye) in the process of killing a Lunar priestess. After the Dragonrise, she returned to her mother's farm to recover.

STR 16	CON 12	SIZ 10
INT 15	DEX 11	CHA 19
POW 14	Magic Points: 14	

Location	D20	Armor/HP
Right Leg	01–04	5/4
Left Leg	05–09	5/4
Abdomen	09–11	3/4
Chest	12	5/5
Right Arm	13–15	5/3
Left Arm	16–18	5/3
Head	19-20	5/4

Weapon	%	Damage	SR	Pts
Broadsword	90	1D8+1+1D4	7	12
Lance	70	1D10+1+3D6	6	10
Battle Axe	55	1D8+2+1D4	7	10
Medium Shield	65	1D6+1D4	7	12
Composite Bow	45	1D8+1	3	7

Runes: Air 90% (Ƨ), Moon 40% (Φ), Earth 20% (□), Death 75% (†), Truth 70% (Y), Movement 75% (≈).

Passions: Hate (Lunar Empire) 90%, Honor 90%, Devotion (Orlanth) 80%, Loyalty (Sartar) 80%, Loyalty (Argrath) 70%, Loyalty (Colymar Tribe) 70%.

Reputation: 20%
Ransom: 500 L.

Move: 8
Damage Bonus: +1D4
Spirit Combat Damage: 1D6+3
Strike Ranks: DEX 3, SIZ 2
Hit Points: 12
Armor: Bronze disk plate cuirass (5 pts.), bronze greaves and vambraces (5 pts.), studded leather skirt (3 pts.), closed helm (5 pts.).
Skills: *Agility:* Dodge 22%, Ride (Bison) 70%. *Communication:* Dance 25%, Fast Talk 15%, Orate 45%, Sing 50%. *Knowledge:* Battle 65%, Cult Lore (Orlanth) 25%, Customs (Heortling) 35%, Farm 30%, First Aid 25%, Herd 20%. Manipulation +5% (includes all weapon skills). *Magic:* Meditate 25%, Spirit Combat 55%, Worship (Orlanth) 35%. *Perception:* Listen 40%, Scan 50%, Search 30%, Track 10%. *Stealth +5%:* Hide 15%, Move Quietly 15%.
Languages: Speak Heortling 60%, Speak Stormspeech 34%, Speak Tradetalk 20%, Read/Write Theyalan 30%, Read/Write New Pelorian 15%.
Rune Points: 3 (Orlanth Adventurous)
Rune Spells: Command Cult Spirit (2), Dark Walk (1), Dismiss Magic (Var.), Dismiss Air Elemental (as per elemental size), Divination (1), Earth Shield (3), Extension 1, Find Enemy 1, Flight (var.), Heal Wound (1), Leap (1), Lightning (var.), Mist Cloud (1), Multispell (1), Shield (var.), Spirit Block (var.), Summon Air Elemental (as per elemental size, see separate write-up), Teleportation (3), Wind Words (1).
Spirit Magic: Mobility (1 pt.), Demoralize (2 pts.), Healing 2.
Magic Items: 10-point magic point storage crystal, piece of raw Truestone.
Treasures: Carries 20 L in coin, armor and helmet, medium shield, broadsword, lance, battle axe, composite bow with 20 arrows, riding bison (see separate write-up).

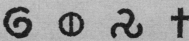

YANIOTH, VAREENA'S DAUGHTER

Apprentice priestess of the Earth goddess Ernalda, member of the Ernaldori clan of the Colymar Tribe. Female, age 23.

Introduction: *Call me Yanioth Vareena's Daughter, and like my mother, you will know me as a priestess of Ernalda. Praised be the Earth and all its secrets! I know the sacred dances of life and lust as well as the rites of birth and renewal. I speak to spirits of the higher worlds and those of the earth, and I know the ways of knitting flesh and bone to their wholeness. With my half-sister Vasana, I ventured to Nochet, and there I earned the blessing and favor of Queen Samastina. Now I travel with her, following the path that my goddess has set before me.*

Yanioth is a voluptuous woman with brown hair with braids that twist like snakes. She wears the traditional vestments of an Ernaldan priestess, and has a tone ranging from lofty to occasionally salacious. Despite this, she is helpful and generous to her friends, and ruthless towards her enemies.

She is Vasana's half-sister, sharing the same mother, Vareena, but with a different father. Yanioth's grandmother died at Grizzly Peak defending the Feathered Horse Queen, and her mother (Vareena, a priestess of Ernalda) stayed completely out of the next twenty years of conflict.

It was a great shock to her mother that Yanioth accompanied her half-sister to Nochet, where she gained the blessing and favor of Queen Samastina. Yanioth was present at the Battle of Pennel Ford, accompanied Argrath to summon Jaldon, and helped acclaim Kallyr Starbrow as Prince.

STR 11	CON 12	SIZ 15
INT 16	DEX 15	CHA 17
POW 15	Magic Points: 15	

Location	D20	Armor/HP
Right Leg	01–04	0/5
Left Leg	05–09	0/5
Abdomen	09–11	0/5
Chest	12	0/6
Right Arm	13–15	0/4
Left Arm	16–18	0/4
Head	19–20	0/5

Weapon	%	Damage	SR	Pts
Dagger	35	1D4+2+1D4	6	6
Battle Axe	55	1D8+2+1D4	5	10
Medium Shield	65	1D6+1D4	6	12
Composite Bow	45	1D8+1	2	7

Runes: Earth (□) 90%, Darkness (●) 40%, Air (ᴳ) 30%, Fertility (Ⅹ) 85%, Beast (▼) 85%.

Passions: Devotion (Ernalda) 80%, Loyalty (Colymar Tribe) 70%, Loyalty (Ernaldori Clan) 70%, Love (Family) 70%, Loyalty (Argrath) 60%, Loyalty (Feathered Horse Queen) 60%, Loyalty (Sartar) 60%, Loyalty (Queen Samastina) 60%, Hate (Lunar Empire) 60%.

Reputation: 26%

Ransom: 1000 L.

Move: 8

Damage Bonus: +1D4

Spirit Combat Damage: 1D6+1

Strike Ranks: DEX 2, SIZ 1

Hit Points: 13

Armor: Priestess robe.

Skills: *Agility:* Dodge 35%, Swim 40%. *Communication:* Dance 65%, Fast Talk 15%, Orate 60%, Sing 70%. *Knowledge:* Area Lore (Dragon Pass) 25%, Battle 35%, Cult Lore (Ernalda) 40%, Customs (Heortling) 30%, Farm 30%, First Aid 50%, Herd 20%, Plant Lore 25%, Manage Household 35%. *Magic:* Meditate 35%, Spirit Combat 70%, Worship (Ernalda) 70%. *Perception:* Insight (Human) 35%, Listen 30%, Scan 30%, Search 30, Track 10%. *Stealth:* Hide 15%, Move Quietly 15%.

Languages: Speak Heortling 60%, Speak Earthspeech 30%, Speak Tradetalk 20%, Read/Write Theyalan 10%.

Rune Points: 4 (Ernalda)

Rune Spells: Absorption (var.), Arouse Passion (1), Charisma (1), Command Cult Spirit (2), Dismiss Magic (var.), Dismiss Earth Elemental (as per elemental size), Divination (1), Earthpower (3), Extension (1), Find Enemy (1), Heal Body (3), Heal Wound (1), Inviolable (1), Multispell (1), Regrow Limb (2), Soul Sight (1), Spirit Block (Var.), Summon Earth Elemental (as per elemental size, see separate write-up).

Spirit Magic: Slow (1 pt.), Heal 3, Befuddle (2 pts.).

Magic Items: 10-point magic point storage crystal.

Treasures: Rich from the favor she received from Queen Samastina in Nochet, Yanioth starts with 640 L in coin, composite bow with 20 arrows, battle axe, dagger, medium shield. At home, she has 1780 L in jewelry, vessels, and luxury goods.

VOSTOR, SON OF PYJEEM

Heavy infantry soldier from Dunstop, in Lunar Tarsh. Male, age 21. Initiate of Seven Mothers.

Introduction: *Hold before you strike, brave adventurers! It is true that I am a Lunar, out of Dunstop in Tarsh, but I have renounced any allegiance to the Lunar Empire, and have chosen to follow a destiny other than that of invader. My name is Vostor. Though I am a deserter, I am no common traitor! I put my kopis-sword and shield to use serving the Red Emperor in Nochet and at the Battle of Pennel Ford, and in his name, I was nearly maimed by the savage called Harek the Berserk. While I recovered, an attempt was made on my life, a purge initiated by the new regime. I had little choice but leave or face assassination or prison, at best. I have found acceptance, even friends, among my former enemies, and now I am my own man, seeking my own path in the world.*

Vostor, Son of Pyjeem, is from a long line of Lunar Tarshite soldiers from Dunstop. He has a thick mop of black hair, piercing eyes, and a powerful physique, but his most noticeable feature is a ragged row of fearsome scars across the right side of his face and his right arm, healed but still testament to the terrible injury he suffered.

Vostor's grandfather fought and died for the Red Emperor at the Battle of Grizzly Peak. Pyjeem followed General Fazzur Wideread but died with great glory in the Hendriking Campaign.

At adulthood, Vostor joined the Dunstop Foot and was shocked when the Red Emperor replaced Fazzur Wideread as the Governor-General of Dragon Pass. Nonetheless, he followed his regiment to Esrolia and fought valiantly in the siege of Nochet. However, the Empire failed to take the city. At the Battle of Pennel Ford Vostor was nearly killed by Harrek the Berserk, gaining the terrible scars across his face and right arm. Vostor returned to Dragon Pass to recover, but during the retreat from Sartar, partisans of King Pharandos tried to assassinate him as part of a purge of those officers who were loyal to Fazzur. Rather than be murdered, Vostor deserted and sought allies amongst his former enemies in Sartar.

STR 16	CON 15	SIZ 13
INT 15	DEX 15	CHA 10
POW 15	Magic Points: 15	

Location	D20	Armor/HP
Right Leg	01–04	6/5
Left Leg	05–09	6/5
Abdomen	09–11	5/5
Chest	12	5/6
Right Arm	13–15	6/4
Left Arm	16–18	6/4
Head	19–20	5/5

Weapon	%	Damage	SR	Pts
Kopis	80	1D8+1+1D4	6	12
Short Spear	45	1D6+1+1D4	6	10
Dagger	45	1D4+2+1D4	7	7
Large Shield	90	1D6+1D4	7	16
Javelin	30	1D10+1D2	2	8
Composite Bow	50	1D8+1	2	7
Medium Shield	35	1D6+1D4	7	12

Runes: Moon 90% (Φ), Air 50% (ᚷ), Earth 50% (□), Disorder 75% (ᛉ), Illusion (∴) 75%.

Passions: Fear (Dragons) 60%, Fear (Harrek the Berserk) 60%, Hate (King Pharandos) 60%, Honor 70%, Love (Family) 60%, Loyalty (Dunstop) 60%, Loyalty (Fazzur Wideread) 80%, Loyalty (Red Emperor) 60%.

Reputation: 19%
Ransom: 500 L.

Move: 8
Damage Bonus: +1D4
Spirit Combat Damage: 1D6+1
Strike Ranks: DEX 2, SIZ 2
Hit Points: 16
Armor: Heavy scale hauberk (5 pts.), plate greaves and vambraces (6 pts.), closed helmet (5 pts.).
Skills: *Agility:* Dodge 35%. *Communication:* Dance 15%, Fast Talk 15%, Oratory 20%, Intrigue 15%, Sing 30%. *Knowledge:* Area Lore (Lunar Tarsh) 25%, Battle 55%, Celestial Lore 15%, Cult Lore (Seven Mothers) 25%, Customs (Lunar Provincial) 40%, Farm 35%, First Aid 30%. Magic +5%: Meditate 15%, Spirit Combat 45%, Worship (Seven Mothers) 35%. *Perception:* Listen 40%, Scan 65%, Search 25%, Track 5%. *Stealth:* Hide 15%, Move Quietly 15%.
Languages: Speak New Pelorian 70/20%, Speak Tarshite 30%, Speak Tradetalk 20%, Speak Heortling 10%.
Rune Points: 3 (Seven Mothers)
Rune Spells: Command Cult Spirit (2), Dismiss Small Elemental (1), Dismiss Magic (var.), Divination (1), Extension (1), Find Enemy (1), Heal Wound (1), Madness (1), Mindblast (2), Multispell (1), Reflection (var.), Regrow Limb (2), Soul Sight (1), Spirit Block (var.), Summon Small Fire Elemental (1) (see separate write-up).
Magic Points: 15
Spirit Magic: Befuddle (2 pts.), Glamour (2 pts.), Heal 1.
Magic Items: A spell matrix for Heal 2 in the form of a belt buckle depicting a fat, grinning dwarf.
Treasures: 125 L in coin and booty, armor and helmet, large shield, kopis, short spear, dagger, two javelins, composite bow with 20 arrows.

SORALA, DAUGHTER OF TORIA

Revolutionary and scribe from Nochet. Female, 21 years old. Initiate of Lhankor Mhy.

Introduction: *Let me be brief here, for I am in the middle of composing a treatise and I do not wish to lose the trail of thought. I am Sorala, a scholar out of the Lhankor Mhy temple in Nochet. My mother taught me in the ways of writing and reading, and instilled in me a great love for the pursuit of knowledge. History, languages, lore, rhetoric, logic, and even the paths of sorcery are among my specialities, and my translations of Second Age Auld Wyrmish brought me great acclaim amidst my peers. But do not think me a mere book-mite or meek copier: I have fought and shed blood for Queen Samastina and King Argrath, and put my sword to work as readily as my stylus! I have joined a small group of adventurers and travel with them now, wishing to explore more of my homeland of Dragon Pass.*

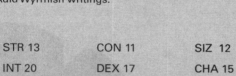

Sorala is an adventurous and athletic scholar, with long brown hair. Her attire is practical and nondescript, aside from the bejeweled veil she wears as a "beard."

Sorala is the granddaughter of a Lhankor Mhy sage at the Nochet Knowledge Temple. He aided the House of Sartar against Lunar Assassins and died with great glory when Belintar raised the Building Wall. Her mother was Toria, also a sage of Lhankor Mhy. She survived the Lion King's Feast but died with great glory during Greymane's Great Raid.

After a lengthy apprenticeship, Sorala was initiated into the Lhankor Mhy. During the civil war in Esrolia, Sorala supported the usurper Samastina, and fought gloriously to protect her from Red Earth assassins. During the siege of Nochet, she was blessed by the Earth Queen, and fought with distinction at the Battle of Pennel Ford. Sorala accompanied Argrath White Bull to Pavis, and acclaimed him as King of Pavis. In Pavis, she befriended Vasana and Yanioth, and accompanied them back to Dragon Pass.

Sorala is a noted sage concerning the Second Age, particularly the city of Old Pavis and of Auld Wyrmish writings.

STR 13	CON 11	SIZ 12
INT 20	DEX 17	CHA 15
POW 13	Magic Points: 13	

Location	D20	Armor/HP
Right Leg	01–04	3/4
Left Leg	05–09	3/4
Abdomen	09–11	3/4
Chest	12	3/5
Right Arm	13–15	3/3
Left Arm	16–18	3/3
Head	19–20	6/4

Weapon	%	Damage	SR	Pts
Broadsword	70	1D8+1+1D4	5	12
Small Axe	35	1D8+2+1D4	5	8
Medium Shield	50	1D6+1D4	6	12
Sling	45	1D8	1	—
Thrown Small Axe	65	1D6+1D3	1	8

Runes: Fire 60% (◎), Air 40% (ᛜ), Earth 20% (▢), Truth 95% (Y), Man 75% (⳹), Harmony 70% (III).

Passions: Hate (Lunar Empire) 60%, Devotion (Lhankor Mhy) 80%, Honor 80%, Loyalty (Queen Samastina) 70%, Loyalty (Argrath) 80%, Loyalty (Family) 60%, Loyalty (Clan) 60%, Loyalty (Nochet) 60%.

Reputation: 18%
Ransom: 1000 L.

Move: 8
Damage Bonus: +1D4
Spirit Combat Damage: 1D6+1
Strike Ranks: DEX 1, SIZ 2
Hit Points: 11
Armor: Linothorax hauberk (3 pts.), cuirboilli greaves and vambraces (3 pts.), full helmet (6 pts.).
Skills: *Agility:* Dodge 44%. *Communication:* Bargain 20%, Dance 30%, Fast Talk 15%, Intrigue 20%, Oratory 30%, Sing 30%. *Knowledge:* Area Lore (Dragon Pass) 25%, Area Lore (Old Pavis) 60%, Battle 50%, Bureaucracy 50%, Cult Lore (Lhankor Mhy) 30%, Farm 45%, Troll Lore 30%, Empire of Wyrm's Friends Lore 35%. *Magic:* Meditate 35%, Spirit Combat 40%, Worship (Lhankor Mhy) 30%. *Perception:* Listen 35%, Scan 35%, Search 35%, Track 15%. *Stealth:* Hide 30%, Move Quietly 30%.
Languages: Speak Esrolian 60%, Speak Heortling 50%, Speak Tradetalk 30%, Read/Write Theyalan 90%, Read/Write Auld Wyrmish 60%, Read/Write New Pelorian 50%.
Rune Points: 3 (Lhankor Mhy)
Rune Spells: Analyze Magic (1), Clairvoyance (1), Command Cult Spirit (2), Detect Truth (1), Dismiss Magic (var.), Divination (1), Extension (1), Find Enemy (1), Heal Wound (1), Knowledge (2), Mind Read (1), Multispell (1), Reconstruction (3), Soul Sight (1), Spirit Block (var.), Translate (1), Truespeak (2).
Spirit Magic: Detect Life, Detect Magic, Detect Spirit, Farsee 2.
Magic Items: Small stone figurine of a crested dragonewt that points in a desired direction (Find Magic matrix).
Treasures: 500 L in coin, jewels, and booty, armor and helmet, broadsword, small axe, medium shield, sling and 10 stones, writing implements and materials; tin disk carved with calendar; letter of introduction from the Knowledge Temple in Nochet.

HARMAST, BARANTHOS' SON

Noble farmer-warrior of the Ernaldori clan of the Colymar Tribe. Male, age 21. Initiate of Issaries.
Introduction: *Harmast is my name, and I am the firstborn son of the great chieftain Baranthos. You have no doubt heard of me. My clan, the Ernaldori, are loyal Sartarites, famed for our prudence and our success. True, my clan defended Colymar tribal lands while others rushed off to war, but when they returned, where were the thanks for our service? I fought in the Battle at Pennel Ford alongside my kinsfolk, and saw the crowning of the Prince of Sartar. My friends and enemies alike know me for a man of words, an envoy and skilled negotiator, but they also know that this fine sword at my side is not for show.*

Harmast is from a noble lineage of the Colymar tribe. His father is the chieftain of the Ernaldori clan, and his grandfather and great-uncle were kings of that tribe. His family are famed for their loyalty to Sartar and for their caution: Harmast's family survived the Lunar Occupation with their lives (and wealth) intact, whereas others of their clan perished.

Harmast was initiated into the cult of Issaries, and tried to avoid the growing conflict in Dragon Pass, preferring talk and negotiation to warfare. However, following the Great Winter, Harmast fought a duel with a thane from the Grey Dog clan and killed him; the thane's kin have sworn vengeance upon Harmast. Harmast fought at the Battle of Pennel Ford, alongside his kinfolk, Vasana and Yanioth. He witnessed the Dragonrise and fought for Starbrow during the Liberation of Sartar, acclaiming her as Prince.

Of average size and appearance, Harmast has close-cropped dark hair and surprisingly bright eyes. His garments and gear are well made and boast ornate decorative motifs, a clear display of his family's wealth. In person he is occasionally a bit arrogant, and quickly defensive when it comes to his choice to remain and defend his family's farm estate when others of his kin answered King Broyan's call.

Harmast is a dealmaker: when he can't make a deal he relies upon his fearsome skills as a duelist. Generally, he tries to remain out of conflicts, but does not hesitate to act decisively when drawn into them.

STR 13	CON 9	SIZ 13
INT 19	DEX 18	CHA 10
POW 16	Magic Points: 16	

Location	D20	Armor/HP
Right Leg	01–04	6/4
Left Leg	05–09	6/4
Abdomen	09–11	6/4
Chest	12	6/5
Right Arm	13–15	6/3
Left Arm	16–18	6/3
Head	19–20	5/4

Weapon	%	Damage	SR	Pts
Broadsword	100	1D8+1+1D4	6	12
Battle Axe	40	1D8+2+1D4	6	10
Dagger	55	1D4+2+1D4	7	
Medium Shield	80	1D6+1D4	6	12
Javelin	45	1D8+1+1D2	1	7

Runes: Air 90% (ᛟ), Fire 45% (◎), Darkness 20% (●), Harmony 90% (III), Movement 75% (ᔕ).
Passions: Hate (Grey Dog) 60%, Love (Family) 80%, Loyalty (Sartar) 80%, Loyalty (Ernaldori Clan) 60%, Loyalty (Colymar Tribe) 60%, Loyalty (Issaries Temple) 60%.
Reputation: 15%
Ransom: 500 L.

Move: 8
Damage Bonus: +1D4
Spirit Combat Damage: 1D6+1
Strike Ranks: DEX 1, SIZ 2
Hit Points: 10
Armor: Plate cuirass (6 pts.), plate greaves and vambraces (6 pts.), closed helmet (5 pts.).
Skills: *Agility:* Dodge 46%, Ride (Horse) 40%. *Communication:* Bargain 65%, Dance 20%, FastTalk 15%, Oratory 50%, Sing 35%. *Knowledge:* Area Lore (Dragon Pass) 30%, Battle 30%, Cult Lore (Issaries) 30%, Customs (Heortling) 70%, Farm 35%, Herd 25%, Manage Household 50%. *Magic +5%:* Meditate 10%, Spirit Combat 65%, Worship (Issaries) 55%. *Perception:* Insight (Human) 60% Listen 35%, Scan 35%, Search 35, Track 15%. *Stealth:* Hide 25%, Move Quietly 30%.
Languages: Speak Heortling 60%, Speak Tradetalk 45%, Read/Write Theyalan 20%.
Rune Points: 3 (Issaries)
Rune Spells: Command Cult Spirit (2), Dismiss Magic (var.), Divination (1), Extension (1), Flight (var.), Find Enemy (1), Heal Wound (1), Multispell (1), Passage (1), Path Watch (2), Safe (2), Soul Sight (1), Spell Trading (2), Spirit Block (var.).
Spirit Magic: Detect Enemy (1 pt.), Farsee (1 pt.), Glamour (2 pts.), Mobility (1 pt.).
Magic Items: Three healing potions that heal 1D10 points of damage each.
Treasures: 150 L in coin, armor and helmet, broadsword, dagger, three javelins, medium shield, two riding zebras.

HARMAST'S ZEBRAS: Harmast rides a Praxian zebra (and has a second), and must dismount to fight, as neither has not been trained to be steady in combat. Each has a Move 12. Characteristics are not needed.

VASANA'S BISON

Vasana rides a trained cavalry bison. When she attacks someone on foot from bison-back, she rolls 1D10+10 to determine hit location. When she uses her lance while charging with her bison, she uses the bison's damage bonus, and not hers!

STR 36	CON 17	SIZ 34
INT N/A	DEX 12	CHA N/A
POW 10	Magic Points: 10	

Location	D20	Armor/HP
Right Hind Leg	01–02	3/6
Left Hind Leg	03–04	3/6
Hindquarters	05–07	3/8
Forequarters	08–10	3/8
Right Front Leg	11–13	3/6
Left Front Leg	14–16	3/6
Head	17–20	3/7

Weapon	%	Damage	SR	Pts
Butt	50	2D10+3D6	8	12
Trample	50	6D6 to downed foe	8	12

Damage Bonus: +3D6
Move: 12
Hit Points: 23
Combat: A bison can butt or trample in the same melee round, not both.
Armor: 3-point hide.

AIR ELEMENTAL

Vasana can spend Rune Points to ask Orlanth to send her any size of air elemental. It will follow her orders and stay in this world for 15 minutes (the duration of the spell) and then dissipate.

Characteristics	Small	Medium	Large
Rune Point cost to summon	1	2	3
SIZ (cubic meters)	27 (3×3×3)	54 (3×6×3)	81 (3×9×3)
Hit Points	10	19	29
STR	10	19	29
POW	11	17	20
Movement	12	12	12

Abilities: An air elemental can carry objects or people with a total SIZ equal to or less than the air elemental's STR. It can create a breeze or a small whirlwind. An air elemental may blow arrows or other missile weapons off course.

Attack: An air elemental attacks by taking a character caught within it and throwing them to the top of the elemental, and then dropping them. Damage is 1D6 plus 1D6 per 3 meters of fall. Thus, a small air elemental can do a maximum of 2D6 damage, but by making the elemental 6 meters high, a medium air elemental can do 3D6 damage, and a large air elemental does 4D6. A character may try to resist by pitting their STR in a resistance roll against the STR of the elemental. If the character resists, they stay on the ground. Characters may choose to attack or cast spells at an air elemental instead of resisting, in hopes that the air elemental will be destroyed in mid-toss, causing only 1/2 damage for the toss. The characters will be tossed, however.

EARTH ELEMENTAL

Yanioth can spend Rune Points to ask Ernalda to send her any size of earth elemental. It will follow her orders and stay in this world for 15 minutes (the duration of the spell) and then dissipate.

Characteristics	Small	Medium	Large
Rune Point cost to summon	1	2	3
SIZ (cubic meters)	27 (3×3×3)	54 (3×6×3)	81 (3×9×3)
Hit Points	10	19	29
STR	10	19	29
POW	11	17	20
Movement	0	1D6	3D6

Abilities: An earth elemental can open pits in the soil, make tunnels, and find buried objects. It can also be used for holding objects stuck into the dirt, keeping loose tunnel roofs from falling, or forming mounds and ridges in the soil (no larger than the elemental's volume). An earth elemental can carry a person and "swim" through the soil if it has STR enough to carry that person. There is no air underground, and an individual being carried must make CON rolls or suffocate. The earth elemental can only do this with an unresisting passenger. An earth elemental can carry several people if its STR is sufficient.

Attack: In combat, the earth elemental uses its volume to engulf its opponents, opening a pit beneath a foe with a maximum volume equal to its own volume. A small earth elemental simply engulfs the victim's legs. A medium earth elemental can swallow victim up to the neck, covering the chest and abdomen as well as the legs. A large earth elemental can swallow its victim completely, engulfing all hit locations. In this case, the victim also will asphyxiate (as per the suffocation rules) unless they break free. After burying a victim, the earth elemental closes up the pit, doing its damage modifier as damage to all hit locations engulfed. An earth elemental can only attack in this manner in dirt or rocky soils (not in sand or soft loam), and can only attack once in a given spot, because the pulverized dirt is too fine for a second attack. The victim is held by the earth elemental in any case, and must overcome the elemental's STR with their own to break free and crawl out of its grip. If an earth elemental lacks any damage bonus, or attacks a victim in unsuitable soil, it will swallow the victim as described above, without causing damage. The victim must still resist STR vs. STR to pull free of the earth elemental's grip.

ELEMENTALS (CONTINUED)

FIRE ELEMENTAL

Vostor can spend 1 Rune Point to ask the Seven Mothers to send him a small fire elemental. It will follow his orders and stay in this world for 15 minutes (the duration of the spell) and then dissipate.

Characteristics	Small
Rune Point cost to summon	1
SIZ (cubic meters)	27 (3×3×3)
Hit Points	10
STR	10
POW	11
Movement	0

Abilities: A fire elemental will ignite any flammable object it touches. It can heat metal (and eventually melt it), bake stone, set fires, and, of course, burn people. Fire elementals float through the air at the same rate as they move on the ground.

Attack: In combat, a fire elemental engulfs its victims in flame. It can engulf 10 SIZ points of enemy per cubic meter of volume. At the end of each round that the victim is engulfed, a roll of 3D6 is matched against the CON of the victim. If the attack is successful, the character takes the 3D6 damage directly to their general hit points. If unsuccessful, 1/2 the amount rolled is applied to the victim's general hit points. Armor will not protect against this damage, but Protection and Shield spells will.

CREDITS

Quickstart Rules and Scenario by
Jeff Richard and Jason Durall

Based on work by
Steve Perrin, Greg Stafford, Sandy Petersen,
Ken Rolston, Ray Turney, and Chris Klug

Cover Art
Andre Fetisov

Illustrations
Roman Kisyov

Proofreading
Andrew Bean

Art Direction
Jeff Richard

Graphic Design & Layout
Nicholas Nacario, Rick Meints, and Michal E. Cross

Cartography
Simon Bray

Play Testing
Andrew Bean, Eric Borg, Barbara Braun, Mara Braun,
Mark Dunleavy, T.F. Druid, Todd Gardiner,
Sven Grottke, Kris Alice Hohls, Claudia Loroff,
Harry O'Brien, Michael O'Brien, Sue O'Brien,
Christine Reich, Neil Robinson, and Jane Saleeba

As always, a special thank you and credit goes to
Greg Stafford, without whom none of us would be reading
this or playing games in Glorantha.

RUNEQUEST
A Chaosium Game
First Edition 1978 (Chaosium)
Second Edition 1979, 1980 (Chaosium)
Third Edition 1984, 1993 (Avalon Hill, Chaosium)
Fourth Edition 2017 (Chaosium)

Copyright ©1978, 1980, 1984, 1993, 2017 by
Moon Design Publications, all rights reserved

RuneQuest, HeroQuest, and Glorantha are trademarks of
Moon Design Publications

Chaosium Inc., 3450 Wooddale Ct, Ann Arbor, MI 48104

CHAOSIUM INC. 2017

978-1-56882-450-5   CHA4027